I0139071

GRACE ABOUNDING TO THE CHIEF OF SINNERS

GRAND TYPE
GRANDTYPECLASSICS.COM

Grace Abounding to the Chief of Sinners
Bunyan, John 1628 – 1688
First Published by George Larkin in 1666

Text edits © 2025 Grand Type Classics
Design © 2025 Grand Type Classics

Text set in 18 point Helvetica.
Chapter headings set in Helvetica Neue.

All rights reserved. All materials in this book are protected by copyright. No part of this publication may be reproduced, distributed, or transmitted in any form or by any means, including photocopying, recording, or other electronic or mechanical methods, without the prior written permission of the publisher.

ISBN: 978-1-83412-264-9

GRACE ABOUNDING TO THE CHIEF OF SINNERS

JOHN BUNYAN

GRAND TYPE CLASSICS

Come and hear all ye that fear God, and I will declare what He hath done for my soul. – Psalm lxvi. 16.

CONTENTS

**Grace Abounding to the Chief
of Sinners**

Prefatory Note

THE TEXT IN THIS edition is as nearly as possible that of the eighth, which was corrected by Bunyan himself a few weeks before his death. The text of 'A Relation' is that of the first edition of 1765. A few minor changes have been introduced for the convenience of the reader. The use of capital letters has been considerably modified, and the orthography has been in places modernized. In some few instances the Scripture references have been added to quotations where they did not appear in the original. It must be remembered that Bunyan often quoted Scripture inexactly, and it has not been deemed necessary to make all his quotations follow the text of the Authorized Version.

The marginal summary is not part of the original, but has been prepared for this edition in order that it may correspond with the Society's editions of the 'Pilgrim's Progress.'[1]

The illustrations have been prepared for this work by Mr. Harold Copping, whose illustrations to the 'Pilgrim's Progress' have justly attracted much attention.

_____

[1]   The marginal summaries have not been included in this Project Gutenberg eText. – DP.

A Preface

OR, BRIEF ACCOUNT OF the publishing this work. Written by the author thereof, and dedicated to those whom God hath counted him worthy to beget to faith, by his ministry in the word.

Children, Grace be with you. **Amen**. I being taken from you in presence, and so tied up that I cannot perform that duty, that from God doth lie upon me to you-ward, for your farther edifying and building up in faith and holiness, etc., yet that you may see my soul hath fatherly care and desire after your spiritual and everlasting welfare, I now once again, as before, from the top of **Shenir** and **Hermon**, so now from **the lions' dens**, **from the mountains of the leopards** (Song iv. 8), do look yet after you all, greatly longing to see your safe arrival into **the** desired Haven.

I thank God upon every remembrance of you; and rejoice, even while I stick between the teeth of the lion in the wilderness, that the grace and mercy, and knowledge of Christ our Saviour, which God hath bestowed upon you, with abundance of faith and love; your hungerings and thirstings after farther acquaintance with the Father, in the Son; your tenderness of heart, your trembling at sin, your sober and holy deportment also, before both God and men, is a great refreshment to me; **For ye are our glory and joy**. 1 Thess. ii. 20.

I have sent you here enclosed, a drop of that honey that I have taken out of the carcase of a lion. Judg. xiv. 5–8. I have eaten thereof myself, and am much refreshed thereby. (Temptations, when we meet them at first, are as the lion that roared upon **Samson**; but if we overcome them, the next time we see them, we shall find a nest of honey within them.) The **Philistines** understand me not. It is something of a relation of the work of God upon my soul, even from the very first, till now, wherein you may perceive my castings down, and risings up: for He woundeth, and His hands make whole. It is written in the Scripture, Isa. xxxviii. 19, **The father to the children shall make known Thy truth**. Yea, it was for this reason I lay so long at Sinai, Lev. iv. 10, 11, to see the fire, and the cloud, and the darkness, **that I might fear the Lord all the days of my life upon earth, and tell of His wondrous works to my children**. Psalm lxxviii. 3–5.

Moses, Numb. xxxiii. 1, 2, writ of the journeys of the children of **Israel**, from

Egypt to the land of **Canaan**; and commanded also that they did remember their forty years' travel in the wilderness. **Thou shalt remember all the way which the Lord thy God led thee these forty years in the wilderness**, **to humble thee**, **and to prove thee**, **and to know what was in thine heart**, **whether thou wouldst keep His commandments**, **or no**. Deut. viii. 2. Wherefore this I have endeavoured to do; and not only so, but to publish it also; that, if God will, others may be put in remembrance of what He hath done for their souls, by reading His work upon me.

It is profitable for Christians to be often calling to mind the very beginnings of grace with their souls. **It is a night to be much observed unto the Lord**, **for bringing them out from the land of Egypt**. **This is that night of the Lord to be observed of all the children of Israel in their generations**. Exod. xii. 42. **O my God** (saith **David**), Ps. xlii. 6, **my soul is**

cast down within me; therefore will I remember thee from the land of Jordan, and of the Hermonites, from the hill Mizar. He remembered also the lion and the bear, when he went to fight with the giant of **Gath**. 1 Sam. xvii. 36, 37.

It was **Paul's** accustomed manner, Acts xxii., and that, when tried for his life, Acts xxiv., even to open before his judges the manner of his conversion: he would think of that day, and that hour, in which he first did meet with grace; for he found it supported him. When God had brought the children of Israel out of the Red Sea, far into the wilderness, yet they must turn quite about thither again, to remember the drowning of their enemies there, Numb. xiv. 25, for though they sang his praise before, yet they soon forgat his works. Psalm cvi. 11, 12.

In this discourse of mine, you may see much; much I say, of the grace of God towards me: I thank God, I can count it much; for it was above my sins and Satan's temptations too. I can remember my fears and doubts, and sad months, with comfort; they are as the head of **Goliah** in my hand: there was nothing to **David** like **Goliah's** sword, even that sword that should have been sheathed in his bowels; for the very sight and remembrance of that did preach forth God's deliverance to him. Oh! the remembrance of my great sins, of my great temptations, and of my great fear of perishing for ever! They bring afresh into my mind, the remembrance of my great help, my great supports from heaven, and the great grace that God extended to such a wretch as I.

My dear children, call to mind the former days, and years of ancient times: remember also your songs in the night, and commune with your own Hearts, Ps. lxxiii. 5–12. Yea, look diligently, and leave no corner therein unsearched for that treasure hid, even the treasure of your first and second experience of the grace of God towards you. Remember, I say, the word that first laid hold upon you:

remember your terrors of conscience, and fear of death and hell: remember also your tears and prayers to God; yea, how you sighed under every hedge for mercy. Have you never a hill **Mizar** to remember? Have you forgot the close, the milk-house, the stable, the barn, and the like, where God did visit your souls? Remember also the word, the word, I say, upon which the Lord hath caused you to hope: if you have sinned against light, if you are tempted to blaspheme, if you are drowned in despair, if you think God fights against you, or if heaven is hid from your eyes; remember it was thus with your father; **but out of them all the Lord delivered me**.

I could have enlarged much in this my discourse, of my temptations and troubles for sin; as also of the merciful kindness and working of God with my soul: I could also have stepped into a style much higher than this, in which I have here discoursed, and could have adorned all things more than here I have seemed to do, but I dare not: God did not play in tempting of me; neither did I play, when I sunk as into the bottomless pit, when the **pangs of hell caught hold upon me**; wherefore I may not play in relating of them, but be plain and simple, and lay down the thing as it was; he that liketh it, let him receive it, and he that doth not, let him produce a better. Farewell.

My dear Children,

The milk and honey are beyond this wilderness. God be merciful to you, and grant that you be not slothful to go in to possess the land.

JOHN BUNYAN.

Grace Abounding
to the Chief of Sinners

or, A Brief Relation Of The Exceeding Mercy Of God In Christ, To His Poor Servant, John Bunyan

IN THIS MY RELATION of the merciful working of God upon my soul, it will not be amiss, if in the first place, I do in a few words give you a hint of my pedigree, and manner of bringing up; that thereby the goodness and bounty of God towards me, may be the more advanced and magnified before the sons of men.

2. For my descent then, it was, as is well known by many, of a low and inconsiderable generation; my father's house being of that rank that is meanest, and most despised of all the families in the land. Wherefore, I have not here, as others, to boast of noble blood, or of any high-born state, according to the flesh; though, all things considered, I magnify the heavenly Majesty, for that by this door He brought me into the world, to partake of the grace and life that is in Christ by the gospel.

3. But yet, notwithstanding the meanness and inconsiderableness of my parents, it pleased God to put it into their hearts, to put me to school, to learn both to read and write; the which I also attained, according to the rate of other poor men's children: though, to my shame, I confess, I did soon

lose that I had learned, even almost utterly, and that long before the Lord did work His gracious work of conversion upon my soul.

4. As for my own natural life, for the time that I was without God in the world, it was, indeed, **according to the course of this world and the spirit that now worketh in the children of disobedience**. Eph. ii. 2, 3. It was my delight to be 'taken captive by the devil **at his will**,' 2 Tim. ii. 26; being filled with all unrighteousness; the which did also so strongly work, and put forth itself, both in my heart and life, and that from a child, that I had but few equals (especially considering my years, which were tender, being but few) both for cursing, swearing, lying, and blaspheming the holy name of God.

5. Yea, so settled and rooted was I in these things, that they became as a second nature to me; the which, as I have also with soberness considered since, did so offend the Lord, that even in my childhood he did scare and affrighten me with fearful dreams, and

did terrify me with fearful visions. For often, after I have spent this and the other day in sin, I have in my bed been greatly afflicted, while asleep, with the apprehensions of devils and wicked spirits, who still, as I then thought, laboured to draw me away with them, of which I could never be rid.

6. Also I should, at these years, be greatly afflicted and troubled with the thoughts of the fearful torments of hell-fire; still fearing, that it would be my lot to be found at last among those devils and hellish fiends, who are there bound down with the chains and bonds of darkness, unto the judgment of the great day.

7. These things, I say, when I was but a child, but nine or ten years old, did so distress my soul, that then in the midst of my many sports and childish vanities, amidst my vain companions, I was often much cast down, and afflicted in my mind therewith, yet could I not let go my sins: yea, I was also then so overcome with despair

of life and heaven, that I should often wish, either that there had been no hell, or that I had been a devil; supposing they were only tormentors; that if it must needs be, that I went thither, I might be rather a tormentor, than be tormented myself.

8. A while after those terrible dreams did leave me, which also I soon forgot; for my pleasures did quickly cut off the remembrance of them, as if they had never been: wherefore with more greediness, according to the strength of nature, I did still let loose the reins of my lust, and delighted in all transgressions against the law of God: so that until I came to the state of marriage, I was the very ringleader of all the youth that kept me company, in all manner of vice and ungodliness.

9. Yea, such prevalency had the lusts and fruits of the flesh in this poor soul of mine, that had not a miracle of precious grace prevented, I had not only perished by the stroke of eternal justice, but had also laid

myself open, even to the stroke of those laws which bring some to disgrace and open shame before the face of the world.

10. In these days the thoughts of religion were very grievous to me; I could neither endure it myself, nor that any other should; so that when I have seen some read in those books that concerned Christian piety, it would be as it were a prison to me. **Then I said unto God, Depart from me, for I desire not the knowledge of Thy ways**. Job xxi. 14, 15. I was now void of all good consideration, heaven and hell were both out of sight and mind; and as for saving and damning, they were least in my thoughts. **O Lord, Thou knowest my life, and my ways were not hid from Thee!**

11. But this I well remember, that though I could myself sin with the greatest delight and ease, and also take pleasure in the vileness of my companions; yet, even then, if I had at any time seen wicked things, by those who professed goodness, it would make my spirit

tremble. As once above all the rest, when I was in the height of vanity, yet hearing one to swear, that was reckoned for a religious man, it had so great a stroke upon my spirit, that it made my heart ache.

12. But God did not utterly leave me, but followed me still, not now with convictions, but judgments; yet such as were mixed with mercy. For once I fell into a creek of the sea, and hardly escaped drowning. Another time I fell out of a boat into **Bedford** river, but, mercy yet preserved me alive: besides, another time, being in a field, with one of my companions, it chanced that an adder passed over the highway, so I having a stick in my hand, struck her over the back; and having stunned her, I forced open her mouth with my stick, and plucked her sting out with my fingers; by which act had not God been merciful unto me, I might by my desperateness, have brought myself to my end.

13. This also I have taken notice of, with

thanksgiving: When I was a soldier, I with others, were drawn out to go to such a place to besiege it; but when I was just ready to go, one of the company desired to go in my room: to which, when I had consented, he took my place; and coming to the siege, as he stood sentinel, he was shot in the head with a musket-bullet and died.

14. Here, as I said, were judgments and mercy, but neither of them did awaken my soul to righteousness; wherefore I sinned still, and grew more and more rebellious against God, and careless of my own salvation.

15. Presently after this, I changed my condition into a married state, and my mercy was, to light upon a wife whose father was counted godly: This woman and I, though we came together as poor as poor might be (not having so much household stuff as a dish or a spoon betwixt us both), yet this she had for her part: **The Plain Man's Pathway to Heaven** and **The Practice of Piety**; which

her father had left her when he died. In these two books I would sometimes read with her, wherein I also found some things that were somewhat pleasing to me (but all this while I met with no conviction). She also would be often telling of me what a godly man her father was, and how he would reprove and correct vice, both in his house, and among his neighbours; what a strict and holy life he lived in his days, both in word and deed.

16. Wherefore these books, with this relation, though they did not reach my heart, to awaken it about my sad and sinful state, yet they did beget within me some desires to religion: so that because I knew no better, I fell in very eagerly with the religion of the times; to wit, to go to church twice a day, and that too with the foremost; and there should very devoutly, both say and sing, as others did, yet retaining my wicked life; but withal, I was so over-run with the spirit of superstition, that I adored, and that with great devotion, even all things (both the high-place, priest, clerk,

vestment, service, and what else) belonging to the church; counting all things holy that were therein contained, and especially, the priest and clerk most happy, and without doubt, greatly blessed, because they were the servants, as I then thought, of God, and were principal in the holy temple, to do His work therein.

17. This conceit grew so strong in a little time upon my spirit, that had I but seen a priest (though never so sordid and debauched in his life), I should find my spirit fall under him, reverence him, and knit unto him; yea, I thought, for the love I did bear unto them (supposing them the ministers of God), I could have laid down at their feet, and have been trampled upon by them; their name, their garb, and work did so intoxicate and bewitch me.

18. After I had been thus for some considerable time, another thought came in my mind; and that was, whether we were of the **Israelites** or no? For finding in the

scripture that they were once the peculiar people of God, thought I, if I were one of this race, my soul must needs be happy. Now again, I found within me a great longing to be resolved about this question, but could not tell how I should: at last I asked my father of it; who told me, **No, we were not**. Wherefore then I fell in my spirit, as to the hopes of that, and so remained.

19. But all this while, I was not sensible of the danger and evil of sin; I was kept from considering that sin would damn me, what religion soever I followed, unless I was found in Christ: nay, I never thought of Him, or whether there was such a One, or no. **Thus man, while blind, doth wander, but wearieth himself with vanity, for he knoweth not the way to the city of God**. Eccles. x. 15.

20. But one day (amongst all the sermons our parson made) his subject was, to treat of the Sabbath day, and of the evil of breaking that, either with labour, sports

or otherwise. (Now, I was, notwithstanding my religion, one that took much delight in all manner of vice, and especially that was the day that I did solace myself therewith): wherefore I fell in my conscience under his sermon, thinking and believing that he made that sermon on purpose to show me my evil doing. And at that time I felt what guilt was, though never before, that I can remember; but then I was, for the present, greatly loaden therewith, and so went home when the sermon was ended, with a great burthen upon my spirit.

21. This, for that instant did benumb the sinews of my best delights, and did imbitter my former pleasures to me; but hold, it lasted not, for before I had well dined, the trouble began to go off my mind, and my heart returned to its old course: but oh! how glad was I, that this trouble was gone from me, and that the fire was put out, that I might sin again without control! Wherefore, when I had satisfied nature with my food, I shook

the sermon out of my mind, and to my old custom of sports and gaming, I returned with great delight.

22. But the same day, as I was in the midst of a game of Cat, and having struck it one blow from the hole, just as I was about to strike it the second time, a voice did suddenly dart from heaven into my soul, which said, **Wilt thou leave thy sins and go to heaven**, **or have thy sins and go to hell**? At this I was put to an exceeding maze; wherefore leaving my cat upon the ground, I looked up to heaven, and was, as if I had, with the eyes of my understanding, seen the Lord Jesus looking down upon me, as being very hotly displeased with me, and as if He did severely threaten me with some grievous punishment for these and other ungodly practices.

23. I had no sooner thus conceived in my mind, but, suddenly, this conclusion was fastened on my spirit (for the former hint did set my sins again before my face), **That I**

had been a great and grievous sinner, and that it was now too late for me to look after heaven; **for Christ would not forgive me**, **nor pardon my transgressions**. Then I fell to musing on this also; and while I was thinking of it, and fearing lest it should be so; I felt my heart sink in despair, concluding it was too late; and therefore I resolved in my mind I would go on in sin: for, thought I, if the case be thus, my state is surely miserable; miserable if I leave my sins, and but miserable if I follow them; I can but be damned, and if I must be so, I had as good be damned for many sins, as be damned for few.

24. Thus I stood in the midst of my play, before all that then were present: but yet I told them nothing: but I say; having made this conclusion, I returned desperately to my sport again; and I well remember, that presently this kind of despair did so possess my soul, that I was persuaded I could never attain to other comfort than what I should get in sin; for heaven was

gone already, so that on that I must not think; wherefore I found within me great desire to take my fill of sin, still studying what sin was yet to be committed, that I might taste the sweetness of it; and I made as much haste as I could to fill my belly with its delicates, lest I should die before I had my desire; for that I feared greatly. In these things, I protest before God, I lye not, neither do I feign this form of speech; these were really, strongly, and with all my heart, my desires: **The good Lord**, **Whose mercy is unsearchable**, **forgive me my transgressions**!

25. And I am very confident, that this temptation of the devil is more usual among poor creatures, than many are aware of, even to over-run the spirits with a scurvy and seared frame of heart, and benumbing of conscience, which frame he stilly and slily supplieth with such despair, that, though not much guilt attendeth souls, yet they continually have a secret conclusion

within them, that there is no hope for them; **for they have loved sins, therefore after them they will go**. Jer. ii. 25, and xviii. 12.

26. Now therefore I went on in sin with great greediness of mind, still grudging that I could not be so satisfied with it, as I would. This did continue with me about a month, or more; but one day, as I was standing at a neighbour's shop window, and there cursing and swearing, and playing the madman, after my wonted manner, there sate within, the woman of the house, and heard me; who, though she also was a very loose and ungodly wretch, yet protested that I swore and cursed at that most fearful rate, that she was made to tremble to hear me; and told me further, **that I was the ungodliest fellow for swearing, that she ever heard in all her life; and that I, by thus doing, was able to spoil all the youth in the whole town, if they come but in my company**.

27. At this reproof I was silenced, and put to secret shame; and that too, as I thought,

before the God of heaven; wherefore, while I stood there, and hanging down my head, I wished with all my heart that I might be a little child again, that my father might learn me to speak without this wicked way of swearing; for, thought I, I am so accustomed to it, that it is in vain for me to think of a reformation; for I thought it could never be.

28. But how it came to pass, I know not; I did from this time forward, so leave my swearing, that it was a great wonder to myself to observe it; and whereas before I knew not how to speak unless I put an oath before, and another behind, to make my words have authority; now I could, without it, speak better, and with more pleasantness than ever I could before. All this while I knew not Jesus Christ, neither did I leave my sports and plays.

29. But quickly after this, I fell into company with one poor man that made profession of religion; who, as I then thought, did talk

pleasantly of the scriptures, and of the matters of religion; wherefore falling into some love and liking to what he said, I betook me to my Bible, and began to take great pleasure in reading, but especially with the historical part thereof; for as for Paul's Epistles, and such like scriptures, I could not away with them, being as yet ignorant, either of the corruptions of my nature, or of the want and worth of Jesus Christ to save me.

30. Wherefore I fell to some outward reformation both in my words and life, and did set the commandments before me for my way to heaven; which commandments I also did strive to keep, and, as I thought, did keep them pretty well sometimes, and then I should have comfort; yet now and then should break one, and so afflict my conscience; but then I should repent, and say, I was sorry for it, and promise God to do better next time, and there get help again; for then I thought I pleased God as well as

any man in **England**.

31. Thus I continued about a year; all which time our neighbours did take me to be a very godly man, a new and religious man, and did marvel much to see such a great and famous alteration in my life and manners; and indeed so it was, though yet I knew not Christ, nor grace, nor faith, nor hope; for, as I have well seen since, had I then died, my state had been most fearful.

32. But, I say, my neighbours were amazed at this my great conversion, from prodigious profaneness, to something like a moral life; and truly, so they well might; for this my conversion was as great, as for Tom of Bethlehem to become a sober man. Now therefore they began to praise, to commend, and to speak well of me, both to my face, and behind my back. Now I was, as they said, become godly; now I was become a right honest man. But oh! when I understood these were their words and opinions of me, it pleased me mighty well. For, though as yet

I was nothing but a poor painted hypocrite, yet, I loved to be talked of as one that was truly godly. I was proud of my godliness, and indeed, I did all I did, either to be seen of, or to be well spoken of, by men: and thus I continued for about a twelvemonth, or more.

33. Now you must know, that, before this, I had taken much delight in ringing, but my **conscience** beginning to be tender, I thought such **practice** was but vain, and therefore forced myself to leave it; yet my mind hankered; wherefore I would go to the steeple-house, and look on, though I durst not ring: but I thought this did not become religion neither; yet I forced myself, and would look on still, but quickly after, I began to think, **how if one of the bells should fall**? Then I chose to stand under a main beam, that lay overthwart the steeple, from side to side, thinking here I might stand sure; but then I should think again, should the bell fall with a swing, it might first hit the wall, and then, rebounding upon me, might

kill me for all this beam; this made me stand in the steeple-door; and now, thought I, I am safe enough; for if the bell should now fall, I can slip out behind these thick walls, and so be preserved notwithstanding.

34. So after this I would yet go to see them ring, but would not go any farther than the steeple-door; but then it came into my head, how if the steeple itself should fall? And this thought (it may for aught I know) when I stood and looked on, did continually so shake my mind, that I durst not stand at the steeple-door any longer, but was forced to flee, for fear the steeple should fall upon my head.

35. Another thing was, my dancing; I was a full year before I could quite leave that; but all this while, when I thought I kept this or that commandment, or did, by word or deed, anything that I thought was good, I had great peace in my conscience, and should think with myself, God cannot choose but be now pleased with me; yea, to relate it in mine own way, I thought no

man in **England** could please God better than I.

36. But poor wretch as I was! I was all this while ignorant of Jesus Christ; and going about to establish my own righteousness; and had perished therein, had not God in mercy showed me more of my state by nature.

37. But upon a day, the good providence of God called me to **Bedford**, to work on my calling; and in one of the streets of that town, I came where there were three or four poor women sitting at a door, in the sun, talking about the things of God; and being now willing to hear them discourse, I drew near to hear what they said, for I was now a brisk talker also myself, in the matters of religion; but I may say, **I heard but understood not**; for they were far above, out of my reach. Their talk was about a new birth, the work of God on their hearts, also how they were convinced of their miserable state by nature; they talked how God had visited their souls

with His love in the Lord Jesus, and with what words and promises they had been refreshed, comforted, and supported, against the temptations of the devil: moreover, they reasoned of the suggestions and temptations of Satan in particular; and told to each other, by which they had been afflicted and how they were borne up under his assaults. They also discoursed of their own wretchedness of heart, and of their unbelief; and did contemn, slight and abhor their own righteousness, as filthy, and insufficient to do them any good.

38. And, methought, they spake as if joy did make them speak; they spake with such pleasantness of scripture language, and with such appearance of grace in all they said, that they were to me, as if they had found a new world; as if they were **people that dwelt alone, and were not to be reckoned among their neighbours**. Numb. xxiii. 9.

39. At this I felt my own heart began to shake, and mistrust my condition to be naught; for I saw that in all my thoughts about religion

and salvation, the new-birth did never enter into my mind; neither knew I the comfort of the word and promise, nor the deceitfulness and treachery of my own wicked heart. As for secret thoughts, I took no notice of them; neither did I understand what Satan's temptations were, nor how they were to be withstood, and resisted, etc.

40. Thus, therefore, when I had heard and considered what they said, I left them, and went about my employment again, but their talk and discourse went with me; also my heart would tarry with them, for I was greatly affected with their words, both because by them I was convinced that I wanted the true tokens of a truly godly man, and also because by them I was convinced of the happy and blessed condition of him that was such a one.

41. Therefore I should often make it my business to be going again and again into the company of these poor people; for I could not stay away; and the more I went amongst

them, the more I did question my condition; and as I still do remember, presently I found two things within me, at which I did sometimes marvel (especially considering what a blind, ignorant, sordid and ungodly wretch but just before I was). The one was a very great softness and tenderness of heart, which caused me to fall under the conviction of what by scripture they asserted, and the other was a great bending in my mind, to a continual meditating on it, and on all other good things, which at any time I heard or read of.

42. By these things my mind was now so turned, that it lay like an horse-leech at the vein, still crying out, **Give**, **Give**, Prov. xxx. 15; yea, it was so fixed on eternity, and on the things about the kingdom of heaven (that is, so far as I knew, though as yet, God knows, I knew but little), that neither pleasures, nor profits, nor persuasions, nor threats, could loose it, or make it let go its hold; and though I may speak it with shame,

yet it is in very deed, a certain truth, it would then have been as difficult for me to have taken my mind from heaven to earth, as I have found it often since, to get again from earth to heaven.

43. One thing I may not omit: There was a young man in our town, to whom my heart before was knit, more than to any other, but he being a most wicked creature for cursing, and swearing, and whoreing, I now shook him off, and forsook his company; but about a quarter of a year after I had left him, I met him in a certain lane, and asked him how he did: he, after his old swearing and mad way, answered, he was well. But, Harry, said I, **why do you curse and swear thus**? **What will become of you**, **if you die in this condition**? He answered me in a great chafe, **What would the devil do for company**, **if it were not for such as I am**?

44. About this time I met with some Ranters' books, that were put forth by some of our countrymen, which books were also highly

in esteem by several old professors; some of these I read, but was not able to make any judgment about them; wherefore as I read in them, and thought upon them (seeing myself unable to judge), I would betake myself to hearty prayer in this manner. **O Lord, I am a fool**, **and not able to know the truth from error**: **Lord, leave me not to my own blindness, either to approve of or condemn this doctrine**; **if it be of God, let me not despise it**; **if it be of the devil, let me not embrace it. Lord, I lay my soul in this matter only at Thy foot, let me not be deceived, I humbly beseech Thee**. I had one religious intimate companion all this while, and that was the poor man I spoke of before; but about this time, he also turned a most devilish Ranter, and gave himself up to all manner of filthiness, especially uncleanness: he would also deny that there was a God, angel, or spirit; and would laugh at all exhortations to sobriety; when I laboured to rebuke his wickedness he would laugh the more, and pretend that he had gone through all religions, and could never light on the right till now. He told me also, that in a little time I should see all professors turn to the ways of the Ranters. Wherefore, abominating those cursed principles, I left his company forthwith, and became to him as great a stranger, as I had been before a familiar.

45. Neither was this man only a temptation to me, but my calling lying in the country, I happened to light into several people's company, who though strict in religion formerly, yet were also swept away by these Ranters. These would also talk with me of their ways, and condemn me as legal and dark; pretending that they only had attained to perfection, that could do what they would and not sin. Oh! these temptations were suitable to my flesh, I being but a young man and my nature in its prime; but God, who had, as I hoped, designed me for better things, kept me in

the fear of His name, and did not suffer me to accept such cursed principles. And blessed be God, Who put it into my heart to cry to Him to be kept and directed, still distrusting my own wisdom; for I have since seen even the effects of that prayer, in His preserving me, not only from Ranting errors, but from those also that have sprung up since. The Bible was precious to me in those days.

46. And now methought, I began to look into the Bible with new eyes, and read as I never did before, and especially the epistles of the apostle St Paul were sweet and pleasant to me; and indeed I was then never out of the Bible, either by reading or meditation; still crying out to God, that I might know the truth, and way to heaven and glory.

47. And as I went on and read, I lighted upon that passage, **To one is given**, **by the Spirit**, **the word of wisdom**; **to another the word knowledge by the same Spirit**; **and to another faith**, etc. 1 Cor. xii. And though,

as I have since seen, that by this scripture the Holy Ghost intends, in special, things extraordinary, yet on me it did then fasten with conviction, that I did want things ordinary, even that understanding and wisdom that other Christians had. On this word I mused, and could not tell what to do, especially this word 'Faith' put me to it, for I could not help it, but sometimes must question, whether I had any faith, or no; but I was loath to conclude, I had no faith; for if I do so, thought I, then I shall count myself a very cast-away indeed.

48. No, said I, with myself, though I am convinced that I am an ignorant sot, and that I want those blessed gifts of knowledge and understanding that other people have; yet at a venture I will conclude, I am not altogether faithless, though I know not what faith is; for it was shewn me, and that too (as I have seen since) by Satan, that those who conclude themselves in a faithless state, have neither rest nor quiet in their souls; and I was loath to fall quite into despair.

49. Wherefore by this suggestion I was, for a while, made afraid to see my want of faith; but God would not suffer me thus to undo and destroy my soul, but did continually, against this my sad and blind conclusion, create still within me such suppositions, insomuch that I could not rest content, until I did now come to some certain knowledge, whether I had faith or no, this always running in my mind, **But how if you want faith indeed**? **But how can you tell you have faith**? And besides, I saw for certain, if I had not, I was sure to perish for ever.

50. So that though I endeavoured at the first to look over the business of Faith, yet in a little time, I better considering the matter, was willing to put myself upon the trial whether I had faith or no. But alas, poor wretch! so ignorant and brutish was I, that I knew not to this day no more how to do it, than I know how to begin and accomplish that rare and curious piece of art, which I never yet saw or considered.

51. Wherefore while I was thus considering, and being put to my plunge about it (for you must know, that as yet I had in this matter broken my mind to no man, only did hear and consider), the tempter came in with this delusion, **That there was no way for me to know I had faith**, **but by trying to work some miracle**; urging those scriptures that seem to look that way, for the enforcing and strengthening his temptation. Nay, one day, as I was between **Elstow** and **Bedford**, the temptation was hot upon me, to try if I had faith, by doing some miracle; which miracle at this time was this, I must say to the **puddles** that were in the horsepads, **Be dry**; and to the **dry places**, **Be you puddles**: and truly one time I was going to say so indeed; but just as I was about to speak, this thought came into my mind; **But go under yonder hedge and pray first**, **that God would make you able**. But when I had concluded to pray, this came hot upon me; That if I prayed, and came

again and tried to do it, and yet did nothing notwithstanding, then to be sure I had no faith, but was a cast-away, and lost; nay, thought I, if it be so, I will not try yet, but will stay a little longer.

52. So I continued at a great loss; for I thought, if they only had faith, which could do so wonderful things, then I concluded, that for the present I neither had it, nor yet for the time to come, were ever like to have it. Thus I was tossed betwixt the devil and my own ignorance, and so perplexed, especially at some times, that I could not tell what to do.

53. About this time, the state and happiness of these poor people at Bedford was thus, **in a kind of a vision**, presented to me, I saw as if they were on the sunny side of some high mountain, there refreshing themselves with the pleasant beams of the sun, while I was shivering and shrinking in the cold, afflicted with frost, snow and dark clouds: methought also, betwixt me

and them, I saw a wall that did compass about this mountain, now through this wall my soul did greatly desire to pass; concluding, that if I could, I would even go into the very midst of them, and there also comfort myself with the heat of their sun.

54. About this wall I bethought myself, to go again and again, still prying as I went, to see if I could find some way or passage, by which I might enter therein: but none could I find for some time: at the last, I saw, as it were, a narrow gap, like a little door-way in the wall, through which I attempted to pass: Now the passage being very strait and narrow, I made many offers to get in, but all in vain, even until I was well-nigh quite beat out, by striving to get in; at last, with great striving, methought I at first did get in my head, and after that, by a sideling striving, my shoulders, and my whole body; then I was exceeding glad, went and sat down in the midst of them, and so was comforted with the light and heat of their sun.

55. Now this mountain, and wall, etc., was thus made out to me: The mountain signified the church of the living God: the sun that shone thereon, the comfortable shining of His merciful face on them that were therein; the wall I thought was the word, that did make separation between the Christians and the world; and the gap which was in the wall, I thought, was Jesus Christ, Who is the way to God the Father. John xiv. 6; Matt. vii. 14. But forasmuch as the passage was wonderful narrow, even so narrow that I could not, but with great difficulty, enter in thereat, it showed me, that none could enter into life, but those that were in downright earnest, and unless also they left that wicked world behind them; for here was only room for body and soul, but not for body and soul and sin.

56. This resemblance abode upon my spirit many days; all which time I saw myself in a forlorn and sad condition, but yet was provoked to a vehement hunger and desire

to be one of that number that did sit in the sunshine: Now also I should pray wherever I was: whether at home or abroad; in house or field; and would also often, with lifting up of heart, sing that of the fifty-first Psalm, **O Lord**, **consider my distress**; for as yet I knew not where I was.

57. Neither as yet could I attain to any comfortable persuasion that I had faith in Christ; but instead of having satisfaction here, I began to find my soul to be assaulted with fresh doubts about my future happiness; especially with such as these, **whether I was elected? But how, if the day of grace should now be past and gone**?

58. By these two temptations I was very much afflicted and disquieted; sometimes by one, and sometimes by the other of them. And first, to speak of that about my questioning my election, I found at this time, that though I was in a flame to find the way to heaven and glory, and though nothing could beat me off from this, yet

this question did so offend and discourage me, that I was, especially sometimes, as if the very strength of my body also had been taken away by the force and power thereof. This scripture did also seem to me to trample upon all my desires; **It is not of him that willeth**, **nor of him that runneth**; **but of God that showeth mercy**. Rom. ix. 16.

59. With this scripture I could not tell what to do: for I evidently saw, unless that the great God, of His infinite grace and bounty, had voluntarily chosen me to be a vessel of mercy, though I should desire, and long, and labour until my heart did break, no good could come of it. Therefore this would stick with me, **How can you tell that you are elected**? **And what if you should not**? **How then**?

60. O Lord, thought I, what if I should not indeed? It may be you are not, said the Tempter; it may be so indeed, thought I. Why then, said Satan, you had as good leave

off, and strive no farther; for if indeed, you should not be elected and chosen of God, there is no talk of your being saved; **For it is not of him that willeth**, **nor of him that runneth**; **but of God that showeth mercy**.

61. By these things I was driven to my wits' end, not knowing what to say, or how to answer these temptations: (indeed, I little thought that Satan had thus assaulted me, but that rather it was my own prudence thus to start the question): for that the elect only attained eternal life; that, I without scruple did heartily close withal; but that myself was one of them, there lay the question.

62. Thus therefore, for several days, I was greatly assaulted and perplexed, and was often, when I have been walking, ready to sink where I went, with faintness in my mind; but one day, after I had been so many weeks oppressed and cast down therewith as I was now quite giving up the ghost of all my hopes of ever attaining life, that sentence fell with weight upon my spirit, **Look at the**

generations of old, and see; **did ever any trust in God, and were confounded**?

63. At which I was greatly lightened, and encouraged in my soul; for thus, at that very instant, it was expounded to me: **Begin at the beginning of Genesis, and read to the end of the Revelations, and see if you can find, that there were ever any that trusted in the Lord, and were confounded**. So coming home, I presently went to my Bible, to see if I could find that saying, not doubting but to find it presently; for it was so fresh, and with such strength and comfort on my spirit, that it was as if it talked with me.

64. Well, I looked, but I found it not; only it abode upon me: Then did I ask first this good man, and then another, if they knew where it was, but they knew no such place. At this I wondered, that such a sentence should so suddenly, and with such comfort and strength, seize, and abide upon my heart; and yet that none could find it (for I

doubted not but that it was in holy scripture).

65. Thus I continued above a year, and could not find the place; but at last, casting my eye upon the **Apocrypha** books, I found it in **Ecclesiasticus**, Eccles. ii. 10. This, at the first, did somewhat daunt me; but because by this time I had got more experience of the love and kindness of God, it troubled me the less, especially when I considered that though it was not in those texts that we call holy and canonical; yet forasmuch as this sentence was the sum and substance of many of the promises, it was my duty to take the comfort of it; and I bless God for that word, for it was of God to me: that word doth still at times shine before my face.

66. After this, that other doubt did come with strength upon me, **But how if the day of grace should be past and gone**? How if you have overstood the time of mercy? Now I remember that one day, as I was walking in the country, I was much

in the thoughts of this, **But how if the day of grace is past**? And to aggravate my trouble, the Tempter presented to my mind those good people of **Bedford**, and suggested thus unto me, that these being converted already, they were all that God would save in those parts; and that I came too late, for these had got the blessing before I came.

67. Now I was in great distress, thinking in very deed that this might well be so; wherefore I went up and down, bemoaning my sad condition; counting myself far worse than a thousand fools for standing off thus long, and spending so many years in sin as I had done; still crying out, Oh! that I had turned sooner! Oh! that I had turned seven years ago! It made me also angry with myself, to think that I should have no more wit, but to trifle away my time, till my soul and heaven were lost.

68. But when I had been long vexed with this fear, and was scarce able to take one

step more, just about the same place where I received my other encouragement, these words broke in upon my mind, **Compel them to come in, that my house may be filled**; **and yet there is room**. Luke xiv. 22, 23. These words, but especially those, **And yet there is room**, were sweet words to me; for truly I thought that by them I saw there was place enough in heaven for me; and moreover, that when the Lord Jesus did speak these words, He then did think of me: and that He knowing that the time would come, that I should be afflicted with fear, that there was no place left for me in His bosom, did before speak this word, and leave it upon record, that I might find help thereby against this vile temptation. This I then verily believed.

69. In the light and encouragement of this word I went a pretty while; and the comfort was the more, when I thought that the Lord Jesus should think on me so long ago, and that He should speak those words on

purpose for my sake; for I did think verily, that He did on purpose speak them to encourage me withal.

70. But I was not without my temptations to go back again; temptations I say, both from Satan, mine own heart, and carnal acquaintance; but I thank God these were outweighed by that sound sense of death, and of the day of judgment, which abode, as it were, continually in my view: I would often also think on **Nebuchadnezzar**; of whom it is said, **He had given him all the kingdoms of the earth**. Dan. v. 18, 19. Yet, thought I, if this great man had all his portion in this world, one hour in hell-fire would make him forget all. Which consideration was a great help to me.

71. I was also made, about this time, to see something concerning the beasts that **Moses** counted clean and unclean: I thought those beasts were types of men; the **clean**, types of them that were the people of God; but the **unclean**, types of

such as were the children of the wicked one. Now I read, that the clean beasts **chewed the cud**; that is, thought I, they show us, we must feed upon the word of God: they also **parted the hoof**. I thought that signified, we must part, if we would be saved, with the ways of ungodly men. And also, in further reading about them, I found, that though we did chew the cud, as the **hare**; yet if we walked with claws, like a dog; or if we did part the hoof, like the **swine**, yet if we did not chew the cud, as the sheep, we were still, for all that, but unclean: for I thought the **hare** to be a type of those that talk of the word, yet walk in the ways of sin; and that the **swine** was like him that parted with his outward pollutions, but still wanteth the word of faith, without which there could be no way of salvation, let a man be never so devout. Deut. xiv. After this, I found by reading the word, that those that must be glorified with Christ in another world **must be called by Him**

here; called to the partaking of a share in His word and righteousness, and to the comforts and first-fruits of His Spirit; and to a peculiar interest in all those heavenly things, which do indeed prepare the soul for that rest, and house of glory, which is in heaven above.

72. Here again I was at a very I great stand, not knowing what to do, fearing I was not called; for, thought I, if I be not called, what then can do me good? None but those who are effectually called inherit the kingdom of heaven. But oh! how I now loved those words that spake of a **Christian's calling**! as when the Lord said to one, **Follow Me**; and to another, **Come after Me**: and oh, thought I, that He would say so to me too: how gladly would I run after Him!

73. I cannot now express with what longings and breathings in my soul, I cried to Christ to call me. Thus I continued for a time, all on a flame to be converted to Jesus Christ; and did also see at that day, such glory in a

converted state, that I could not be contented without a share therein. Gold! could it have been gotten for gold, what would I have given for it? Had I had a whole world, it had all gone ten thousand times over for this, that my soul might have been in a converted state.

74. How lovely now was every one in my eyes, that I thought to be converted men and women. They shone, they walked like a people that carried the broad seal of heaven about them. Oh! I saw the lot was fallen to them in pleasant places, and they had a goodly heritage. Psalm xvi. But that which made me sick, was that of Christ, in St Mark, **He goeth up into a mountain, and calleth unto Him whom He would, and they came unto Him**. Mark iii. 13.

75. This scripture made me faint and fear, yet it kindled fire in my soul. That which made me fear, was this; lest Christ should have no liking to me, for He called **whom He would**. But oh! the glory that I saw in

that condition, did still so engage my heart, that I could seldom read of any that Christ did call, but I presently wished, **Would I had been in their clothes, would I had been born Peter; would I had been born John; or, would I had been by and had heard Him when He called them, how would I have cried, O Lord, call me also! But, oh! I feared He would not call me.**

76. And truly, the Lord let me go thus many months together, and shewed me nothing; either that I was already, or should be called hereafter: but at last after much time spent, and many groans to God, that I might be made partaker of the holy and heavenly calling; that word came in upon me: **I will cleanse their blood, that I have not cleansed, for the Lord dwelleth in Zion.** Joel iii. 21. These words I thought were sent to encourage me to wait still upon God; and signified unto me, that if I were not already, yet time might come, I might be in truth converted unto Christ.

77. About this time I began to break my mind to those poor people in **Bedford**, and to tell them my condition; which when they had heard, they told Mr Gifford of me, who himself also took occasion to talk with me, and was willing to be well persuaded of me, though I think from little grounds: but he invited me to his house, where I should hear him confer with others, about the dealings of God with their souls; from all which I still received more conviction, and from that time began to see something of the vanity and inward wretchedness of my wicked heart; for as yet I knew no great matter therein; but now it began to be discovered unto me, and also to work at that rate as it never did before. Now I evidently found, that lusts and corruptions put forth themselves within me, in wicked thoughts and desires, which I did not regard before; my desires also for heaven and life began to fail; I found also, that whereas before my soul was full of longing after God, now it began to hanker after every foolish

vanity; yea, my heart would not be moved to mind that which was good; it began to be careless, both of my soul and heaven; it would now continually hang back, both to, and in every duty; and was as a clog on the leg of a bird, to hinder me from flying.

78. Nay, thought I, now I grow worse and worse: now I am farther from conversion than ever I was before. Wherefore I began to sink greatly in my soul, and began to entertain such discouragement in my heart, as laid me as low as hell. If now I should have burned at the stake, I could not believe that Christ had love for me: alas! I could neither hear Him, nor see Him, nor feel Him, nor favour any of His things; I was driven as with a tempest, my heart would be unclean, and the **Canaanites** would dwell in the land.

79. Sometimes I would tell my condition to the people of God; which, when they heard, they would pity me, and would tell me of the promises; but they had as good have told me, that I must reach the sun with my

finger, as have bidden me receive or rely upon the promises: and as soon I should have done it. All my sense and feeling were against me; and I saw I had an heart that would sin, and that lay under a law that would condemn.

80. These things have often made me think of the child which the father brought to Christ, **who, while he was yet coming to Him, was thrown down by the devil, and also so rent and torn by him, that he lay down and wallowed, foaming**. Luke ix. 42; Mark ix. 20.

81. Further, in these days, I would find my heart to shut itself up against the Lord, and against His holy word: I have found my unbelief to set, as it were, the shoulder to the door, to keep Him out; and that too even then, when I have with many a bitter sigh, cried, Good Lord, break it open: **Lord, break these gates of brass, and cut these bars of iron asunder**. Psalm cvii. 16. Yet that word would sometimes create

in my heart a peaceable pause, **I girded thee**, **though thou hast not known Me**. Isaiah xlv. 5.

82. But all this while, as to the act of sinning, I was never more tender than now: my hinder parts were inward: I durst not take a pin or stick, though but so big as a straw; for my conscience now was sore, and would smart at every touch: I could not now tell how to speak my words, for fear I should misplace them. Oh, how gingerly did I then go, in all I did or said! I found myself as on a miry bog, that shook if I did but stir, and was, as there, left both of God and Christ, and the Spirit, and all good things.

83. But I observed, though I was such a great sinner before conversion, yet God never much charged the guilt of the sins of my ignorance upon me; only He showed me, I was lost if I had not Christ, because I had been a sinner: I saw that I wanted a perfect righteousness to present me without

fault before God, and this righteousness was no where to be found, but in the Person of Jesus Christ.

84. But my original and inward pollution; That, that was my plague and affliction, that I saw at a dreadful rate, always putting forth itself within me; that I had the guilt of, to amazement; by reason of that, I was more loathsome in mine own eyes than was a toad, and I thought I was so in God's eyes too: Sin and corruption, I said, would as naturally bubble out of my heart, as water would bubble out of a fountain: I thought now, that every one had a better heart than I had; I could have changed heart with any body; I thought none but the devil himself could equalise me for inward wickedness and pollution of mind. I fell therefore at the sight of my own vileness deeply into despair; for I concluded, that this condition that I was in, could not stand with a state of grace. Sure, thought I, I am forsaken of God; sure, I am given up to the devil, and

to a reprobate mind: and thus I continued a long while, even for some years together.

85. While I was thus afflicted with the fears of my own damnation, there were two things would make me wonder; the one was, when I saw old people hunting after the things of this life, as if they should live here always: the other was, when I found professors much distressed and cast down, when they met with outward losses; as of husband, wife, child, etc. Lord, thought I, what a-do is here about such little things as these! What seeking after carnal things, by some, and what grief in others for the loss of them! if they so much labour after, and shed so many tears for the things of this present life, how am I to be bemoaned, pitied, and prayed for! My soul is dying, my soul is damning. Were my soul but in a good condition, and were I but sure of it, ah! how rich should I esteem myself, though blessed but with bread and water! I should count those but small afflictions, and should bear

them as little burthens. **A wounded spirit who can bear**!

86. And though I was much troubled, and tossed, and afflicted, with the sight and sense and terror of my own wickedness, yet I was afraid to let this sight and sense go quite off my mind: that unless guilt of conscience was taken off the right way, that is, by the blood of Christ a man grew rather worse for the loss of his trouble of mind, than better. Wherefore, if my guilt lay hard upon me, then I should cry that the blood of Christ might take it off: and if it was going off without it (for the sense of sin would be sometimes as if it would die, and go quite away), then I would also strive to fetch it upon my heart again, by bringing the punishment of sin in hell fire upon my spirit; and should cry, **Lord**, **let it not go off my heart**, **but the right way**, **by the blood of Christ**, **and the application of Thy mercy**, **through Him**, **to my soul**, for that scripture lay much upon me, **without shedding of blood is no remission**. Heb.

ix. 22. And that which made me the more afraid of this, was, because I had seen some, who though when they were under wounds of conscience, would cry and pray; yet seeking rather present ease from their trouble, than pardon for their sin, cared not how they lost their guilt, so they got it out of their mind: now, having got it off the wrong way, it was not sanctified unto them; but they grew harder and blinder, and more wicked after their trouble. This made me afraid, and made me cry to God the more, that it might not be so with me.

87. And now I was sorry that God had made me man, for I feared I was a reprobate; I counted man as unconverted, the most doleful of all the creatures. Thus being afflicted and tossed about my sad condition, I counted myself alone, and above the most of men unblessed.

88. Yea, I thought it impossible that ever I should attain to so much goodness of heart, as to thank God that He had made

me a man. Man indeed is the most noble by creation, of all creatures in the visible world; but by sin he has made himself the most ignoble. The beasts, birds, fishes, etc. I blessed their condition; for they had not a sinful nature; they were not obnoxious to the wrath of God; they were not to go to hell-fire after death; I could therefore have rejoiced, had my condition been as any of theirs.

89. In this condition I went a great while, but when comforting time was come, I heard one preach a sermon on these words in the song, Song iv. 1, **Behold, thou art fair, my love, behold, thou art fair**. But at that time he made these two words, **my love**, his chief and subject matter: from which, after he had a little opened the text, he observed these several conclusions: 1. **That the church, and so every saved soul, is Christ's love, when loveless**. 2. **Christ's love without a cause**. 3. **Christ's love, when hated of the world**. 4. **Christ's love, when under**

temptation and under destruction. 5. Christ's love, from first to last.

90. But I got nothing by what he said at present; only when he came to the application of the fourth particular, this was the word he said; **If it be so, that the saved soul is Christ's love, when under temptation and desertion; then poor tempted soul, when thou art assaulted, and afflicted with temptations, and the hidings of God's face, yet think on these two words**, 'My love,' **still**.

91. So as I was going home, these words came again into my thoughts; and I well remember, as they came in, I said thus in my heart, **What shall I get by thinking on these two words**? This thought had no sooner passed through my heart, but these words began thus to kindle in my spirit, **Thou art My Love, thou art My Dove**, twenty times together; and still as they ran in my mind, they waxed stronger and warmer, and began to make me look up;

but being as yet, between hope and fear, I still replied in my heart, **But is it true, but is it true**? At which that sentence fell upon me, **He wist not that it was true, which was done by the Angel**. Acts xii. 9.

92. Then I began to give place to the word which with power, did over and over make this joyful sound within my soul, '**Thou art my Love, thou art My Love, and nothing shall separate thee from My Love**. And with that my heart was filled full of comfort and hope, and now I could believe that my sins should be forgiven me; yea, I was now so taken with the love and mercy of God, that I remember I could not tell how to contain till I got home: I thought I could have spoken of His love, and have told of His mercy to me, even to the very crows, that sat upon the ploughed lands before me, had they been capable to have understood me: wherefore I said in my soul, with much gladness, **Well, I would I had a pen and ink here, I would write this down before I**

go any farther; **for surely I will not forget this forty years hence**. But, alas! within less than forty days I began to question all again; which made me begin to question all still.

93. Yet still at times I was helped to believe, that it was a true manifestation of grace unto my soul, though I had lost much of the life and favour of it. Now about a week or a fortnight after this I was much followed by this scripture, **Simon**, **Simon**; **behold**, **Satan hath desired to have you**, Luke xxii. 31, and sometimes it would sound so loud within me, yea, and as it was, call so strongly after me, that once, above all the rest, I turned my head over my shoulder, thinking verily that some man had behind me, called me; being at a great distance, methought he called so loud: it came, as I have thought since, to have stirred me up to prayer, and to watchfulness: it came to acquaint me, that a cloud and a storm was coming down upon me: but I understood it not.

94. Also, as I remember, that time that it called to me so loud, was the last time that it sounded in mine ears; but me thinks I hear still with what a loud voice these words, **Simon**, **Simon**, sounded in mine ears. I thought verily, as I have told you, that somebody had called after me, that was half a mile behind me: and although that was not my name, yet it made me suddenly look behind me, believing that he that called so loud, meant me.

95. But so foolish was I, and ignorant, that I knew not the reason of this sound; (which as I did both see and feel soon after, was sent from heaven as an alarm, to awaken me to provide for what was coming,) only I should muse and wonder in my mind, to think what should be the reason of this scripture, and that at this rate, so often and so loud, should still be sounding and rattling in mine ears: but, as I said before, I soon after perceived the end of God therein.

96. For, about the space of a month after,

a very great storm came down upon me, which handled me twenty times worse than all I had met with before; it came stealing upon me, now by one piece, then by another: First, all my comfort was taken from me; then darkness seized upon me; after which, whole floods of blasphemies, both against God, Christ, and the scriptures, were poured upon my spirit, to my great confusion and astonishment. These blasphemous thoughts were such as stirred up questions in me against the very being of God, and of His only beloved Son: As, whether there were in truth, a God or Christ? And whether the holy scriptures were not rather a fable, and cunning story, than the holy and pure word of God?

97. The tempter would also much assault me with this, **How can you tell but that the** Turks **had as good scriptures to prove their** Mahomet **the Saviour, as we have to prove our Jesus is? And, could I think, that so many ten thousands, in so many**

countries and kingdoms, should be without the knowledge of the right way to heaven, (if there were indeed a heaven); and that we only, who live in a corner of the earth, should alone be blessed therewith? Every one doth think his own religion rightest, both Jews **and** Moors, **and** Pagans; **and how if all our faith, and Christ, and scriptures, should be but a think so too**?

98. Sometimes I have endeavoured to argue against these suggestions, and to set some of the sentences of blessed **Paul** against them; but alas! I quickly felt, when I thus did, such arguings as these would return again upon me, **Though we made so great a matter of Paul, and of his words, yet how could I tell, but that in very deed, he being a subtle and cunning man, might give himself up to deceive with strong delusions: and also take the pains and travel, to undo and destroy his fellows.**

99. These suggestions, (with many others

which at this time I may not, and dare not utter, neither by word or pen,) did make such a seizure upon my spirit, and did so overweigh my heart, both with their number, continuance, and fiery force, that I felt as if there were nothing else but these from morning to night within me; and as though indeed there could be room for nothing else; and also concluded, that God had, in very wrath to my soul, given me up to them, to be carried away with them, as with a mighty whirlwind.

100. Only by the distaste that they gave unto my spirit, **I felt there was something in me that refused to embrace them**. But this consideration I then only had, when God gave me leave to swallow my spittle; otherwise the noise, and strength, and force of these temptations would drown and overflow, and as it were, bury all such thoughts, or the remembrance of any such thing. While I was in this temptation, I often found my mind suddenly put upon it to curse

and swear, or to speak some grievous thing against God, or Christ His Son, and of the scriptures.

101. Now I thought, **surely I am possessed of the devil**: at other times, again, I thought I should be bereft of my wits; for instead of lauding and magnifying God the Lord, with others, if I have but heard Him spoken of, presently some most horrible blasphemous thought or other would bolt out of my heart against Him; so that whether I did think that God was, or again did think there was no such thing, no love, nor peace, nor gracious disposition could I feel within me.

102. These things did sink me into very deep despair; for I concluded that such things could not possibly be found amongst them that loved God. I often, when these temptations had been with force upon me, did compare myself to the case of such a child, whom some gipsy hath by force took up in her arms, and is carrying from friend and country. Kick sometimes I did, and also

shriek and cry; but yet I was bound in the wings of the temptation, and the wind would carry me away. I thought also of Saul, and of the evil spirit that did possess him: and did greatly fear that my condition was the same with that of his. 1 Sam. x.

103. In these days, when I have heard others talk of what was the sin against the Holy Ghost, then would the tempter so provoke me to desire to sin that against sin, that I was as if I could not, must not, neither should be quiet until I had committed it; now no sin would serve but that. If it were to be committed by speaking of such a word, then I have been as if my mouth would have spoken that word, whether I would or no; and in so strong a measure was this temptation upon me, that often I have been ready to clap my hand under my chin, to hold my mouth from opening; and to that end also, I have had thoughts at other times, to leap with my head downward, into some muckhill-hole or other, to keep my mouth

from speaking.

104. Now again I beheld the condition of the dog and toad, and counted the estate of every thing that God had made, far better than this dreadful state of mine, and such as my companions were. Yea, gladly would I have been in the condition of a dog or horse: for I knew they had no souls to perish under the everlasting weight of hell, or sin, as mine was like to do. Nay, and though I saw this, felt this, and was broken to pieces with it; yet that which added to my sorrow was, I could not find, that with all my soul I did desire deliverance. That scripture did also tear and rend my soul in the midst of these distractions, **The wicked are like the troubled sea**, **when it cannot rest**, **whose waters cast up mire and dirt**. **There is no peace**, **saith my God**, **to the wicked**. Isa. lvii. 20, 21.

105. And now my heart was, at times, exceeding hard; if I would have given a thousand pounds for a tear, I could not shed

one: no nor sometimes scarce desire to shed one. I was much dejected, to think that this would be my lot. I saw some could mourn and lament their sin; and others again, could rejoice and bless God for Christ; and others again, could quietly talk of, and with gladness remember the word of God; while I only was in the storm or tempest. This much sunk me, I thought my condition was alone, I should therefore much bewail my hard hap, but get out of, or get rid of these things, I could not.

106. While this temptation lasted, which was about a year, I could attend upon none of the ordinances of God, but with sore and great affliction. Yea, then I was most distressed with blasphemies. If I had been hearing the word, then uncleanness, blasphemies and despair would hold me a captive there: if I have been reading, then sometimes I had sudden thoughts to question all I read: sometimes again, my mind would be so strangely snatched away, and possessed with other things, that I have neither known,

nor regarded, nor remembered so much as the sentence that but now I have read.

107. In prayer also I have been greatly troubled at this time; sometimes I have thought I have felt him behind me pulling my clothes: he would be also continually at me in time of prayer, to have done, break off, make haste, you have prayed enough, and stay no longer; still drawing my mind away. Sometimes also he would cast in such wicked thoughts as these; that I must pray to him, or for him: I have thought sometimes of that, **Fall down**; or, **if thou wilt fall down and worship me**. Matt. iii. 9.

108. Also, when because I have had wandering thoughts in the time of this duty, I have laboured to compose my mind, and fix it upon God; then with great force hath the tempter laboured to distract me, and confound me, and to turn away my mind, by presenting to my heart and fancy, the form of a bush, a bull, a besom, or the like, as if

I should pray to these: To these he would also (at sometimes especially) so hold my mind, that I was as if I could think of nothing else, or pray to nothing else but to these, or such as they.

109. Yet at times I should have some strong and heart-affecting apprehensions of God, and the reality of the truth of His gospel. But, oh! how would my heart, at such times, put forth itself with unexpressible groanings. My whole soul was then in every word; I should cry with pangs after God, that He would be merciful unto me; but then I should be daunted again with such conceits as these: I should think that God did mock at these my prayers, saying, and that in the audience of the holy angels, **This poor simple wretch doth hanker after Me, as if I had nothing to do with My mercy, but to bestow it on such as he. Alas, poor soul! how art thou deceived! It is not for such as thee to have favour with the Highest**.

110. Then hath the tempter come upon me, also, with such discouragements as these: **You are very hot for mercy, but I will cool you**; **this frame shall not last always**: **many have been as hot as you for a spurt, but I have quenched their zeal** (and with this, such and such, who were fallen off, would be set before mine eyes). Then I should be afraid that I should do so too: But, thought I, I am glad this comes into my mind: well, I will watch, and take what care I can. **Though you do**, said Satan, **I shall be too hard for you**; **I will cool you insensibly, by degrees, by little and little. What care I**, saith he, **though I be seven years in chilling your heart, if I can do it at last? Continual rocking will lull a crying child asleep: I will ply it close**, **but I will have my end accomplished. Though you be burning hot at present, I can pull you from this fire; I shall have you cold before it be long**.

111. These things brought me into great

straits; for as I at present could not find myself fit for present death, so I thought, to live long, would make me yet more unfit; for time would make me forget all, and wear even the remembrance of the evil of sin, the worth of heaven, and the need I had of the blood of Christ to wash me, both out of mind and thought: but I thank Christ Jesus, these things did not at present make me slack my crying, but rather did put me more upon it (**like her who met with adulterer**, Deut. xxii. 26), in which days that was a good word to me, after I had suffered these things a while: – **I am persuaded that neither death**, **nor life**, **etc.**, **shall be able to separate us from the love of God which is in Christ Jesus our Lord**. Rom. viii. 38, 39. And now I hoped long life would not destroy me, nor make me miss of heaven.

112. Yet I had some supports in this temptation, though they were then all questioned by me; that in **Jer. iii.** at the first was something to me; and so was the

consideration of verse 5 of that chapter; that though we have spoken and done as evil things as we could, yet we should cry unto God, **My Father**, **Thou art the Guide of my youth**, and shall return unto Him.

113. I had, also, once a sweet glance from that in 2 Cor. v. 21: **For He hath made Him to be sin for us**, **Who knew no sin**, **that we might be made the righteousness of God in Him**. I remember that one day, as I was sitting in a neighbour's house, and there very sad at the consideration of my many blasphemies; and as I was saying in my mind, **What ground have I to say that**, **who have been so vile and abominable**, **should ever inherit eternal life**? That word came suddenly upon me, **What shall we say to these things**? **If God be for us**, **who can be against us**? Rom. viii. 31. That also was an help unto me, **Because I live**, **ye shall live also**. John xiv. 19. But these words were but hints, touches, and short visits, though very sweet when

present; only they lasted not; but, **like to** Peter's **sheet, of a sudden were caught up from me, to heaven again**. Acts x. 16.

114. But afterwards the Lord did more fully and graciously discover Himself unto me, and indeed, did quite, not only deliver me from the guilt that, by these things was laid upon my conscience, but also from the very filth thereof; for the temptation was removed, and I was put into my right mind again, as other Christians were.

115. I remember that one day, as I was travelling into the country, and musing on the wickedness and blasphemy of my heart, and considering the enmity that was in me to God, that scripture came into my mind, **Having made peace through the blood of His cross**. Col. i. 20. By which I was made to see, both again and again, that God and my soul were friends by His blood; yea, I saw that the justice of God, and my sinful soul could embrace and kiss each other, through His blood. This was a good day to me; I hope

I shall never forget it.

116. At another time, as I sat by the fire in my house, and was musing on my wretchedness, the Lord made that also a precious word unto me, **Forasmuch then as the children are partakers of flesh and blood, He also Himself likewise took part of the same, that through death He might destroy him that had the power of death, that is the devil; and deliver those who through fear of death, were all their lifetime subject to bondage**. Heb. ii. 14, 15. I thought that the glory of these words was then so weighty on me, that I was both once and twice ready to swoon as I sate; yet not with grief and trouble, but with solid joy and peace.

117. At this time also I sate under of holy Mr **Gifford**, whose doctrine, by God's grace, was much for my stability. This man made it much his business to deliver the people of God from all those false and unsound tests, that by nature we are prone to. He would bid us take special heed, that we

took not up any truth upon trust; as from this, or that, or any other man or men; but to cry mightily to God, that He would convince us of the reality thereof, and set us down therein by His own Spirit in the holy word; **For**, said he, **if you do otherwise, when temptations come**, **if strongly**, **you not having received them with evidence from heaven, will find you want that help and strength now to resist, that once you thought you had**.

118. This was as seasonable to my soul, as the former and latter rains in their season (for I had found, and that by sad experience, the truth of these his words: for I had felt **no man can say**, especially when tempted by the devil, **that Jesus Christ is Lord, but by the Holy Ghost**). Wherefore I found my soul, through grace, very apt to drink in this doctrine, and to incline to pray to God, that in nothing that pertained to God's glory, and my own eternal happiness, He would suffer me to be without the confirmation thereof from

heaven; for now I saw clearly, there was an exceeding difference betwixt the notion of the flesh and blood, and the revelations of God in heaven: also a great difference betwixt that faith that is feigned, and according to man's wisdom, and that which comes by a man's being born thereto of God. Matt. xvi. 15; 1 John v. 1.

119. But, oh! now, how was my soul led from truth to truth by God! Even from the birth and cradle of the Son of God, to His accession, and second coming from heaven to judge the world!

120. Truly, I then found, upon this account, the great God was very good unto me; for, to my remembrance, there was not any thing that I then cried unto God to make known, and reveal unto me, but He was pleased to do it for me; I mean, not one part of the gospel of the Lord Jesus, but I was orderly led into it: methought I saw with great evidence, from the relation of the four evangelists, the wonderful work

of God, in giving Jesus Christ to save us, from His conception and birth, even to His second coming to judgment: methought I was as if I had seen Him born, as if I had seen Him grow up; as if I had seen Him walk through this world, from the cradle to the cross; to which also, when He came, I saw how gently He gave Himself to be hanged, and nailed on it for my sins and wicked doings. Also as I was musing on this His progress, that dropped on my spirit, **He was ordained for the slaughter**. 1 Peter i. 12, 20.

121. When I have considered also the truth of His resurrection, and have remembered that word, **Touch Me not**, **Mary**, etc., I have seen as if He had leaped out of the grave's mouth, for joy that He was risen again, and had got the conquest over our dreadful foes. John xx. 17. I have also in the spirit, seen Him a man, on the right hand of God the Father for me; and have seen the manner of His coming from heaven, to judge the

world with glory, and have been confirmed in these things by these scriptures following, Acts i. 9, 10, and vii. 56, and x. 42; Heb. vii. 24 and ix. 28; Rev. i. 18; 1 Thess. iv. 17, 18.

112. Once I was troubled to know whether the Lord Jesus was man as well as God, and God as well as man: and truly, in those days, let men say what they would, unless I had it with evidence from heaven, all was nothing to me; I counted myself not set down in any truth of God. Well, I was much troubled about this point, and could not tell how to be resolved; at last, that in Rev. v. 6 came into my mind: **And I beheld**, **and**, **to**, **in the midst of the throne**, **and of the four beasts**, **and in the midst of the elders**, **stood a Lamb**, **as it had been slain**. In the midst of the throne, thought I, there is the Godhead; in the midst of the elders, there is His manhood; but, oh! methought this did glister! It was a goodly touch, and gave me sweet satisfaction. That other scripture also did help me much in this, **For unto us**

a Child is born, **unto us a Son is given**; **and the government shall be upon His shoulder**: **and His name shall be called Wonderful**, **Counsellor**, **the Mighty God**, **the Everlasting Father**, **the Prince of Peace**, etc. Isa. ix. 6.

123. Also besides these teachings of God in His word, the Lord made use of two things to confirm me in this truth; the one was the errors of the Quakers and the other was the guilt of sin; for as the Quakers did oppose this truth, so God did the more confirm me in it, by leading me into the scripture that did wonderfully maintain it.

124. The errors that this people then maintained, were: –

1. That the holy scriptures were not the word of God.
2. That every man in the world had the spirit of Christ, grace, faith, etc.
3. That Christ Jesus, as crucified, and dying sixteen hundred years ago, did not satisfy divine justice for the sins of

the people.

4. That Christ's flesh and blood were within the saints.

5. That the bodies of the good and bad that are buried in the church-yard, shall not arise again.

6. That the resurrection is past with good men already.

7. That that man Jesus, that was crucified between two thieves, on mount **Calvary**, in the land of **Canaan**, by **Jerusalem**, was not ascended above the starry heavens.

8. That He should not, even the same Jesus that died by the hands of the Jews, come again at the last day; and as man, judge all nations,' etc.

125. Many more vile and abominable things were in those days fomented by them, by which I was driven to a more narrow search of the scriptures, and was through their light and testimony, not only enlightened, but greatly confirmed and comforted in the

truth: And, as I said, the guilt of sin did help me much; for still as that would come upon me, the blood of Christ did take it off again, and again, and again; and that too sweetly, according to the scripture. **O friends! cry to God to reveal Jesus Christ unto you; there is none teacheth like Him**.

126. It would be too long here to stay, to tell you in particular, how God did set me down in all the things of Christ, and how He did, that He might so do, lead me into His words; yea, and also how He did open them unto me, and make them shine before me, and cause them to dwell with me, talk with me, and comfort me over and over, both of His own being, and the being of His Son, and Spirit, and word, and gospel.

127. Only this, as I said before, I will say unto you again, that in general, He was pleased to take this course with me; first, to suffer me to be afflicted with temptations concerning them, and then reveal them unto me; as sometimes I should lie under great

guilt for sin, even crushed to the ground therewith; and then the Lord would show me the death of Christ; yea, so sprinkle my conscience with His blood, that I should find, and that before I was aware, that in that conscience, where but just now did reign and rage the law, even there would rest and abide the peace and love of God, through Christ.

128. Now I had an evidence, as I thought, of my salvation, from heaven, with many golden seals thereon, all hanging in my sight. Now could I remember this manifestation, and the other discovery of grace, with comfort; and should often long and desire that the last day were come, that I might be for ever inflamed with the sight, and joy, and communion of Him, Whose head was crowned with thorns, Whose face was spit upon, and body broken, and soul made an offering for my sins. For whereas before I lay continually trembling at the mouth of hell, now methought I was

got so far therefrom, that I could not, when I looked back, scarce discern it! And oh! thought I, that I were fourscore years old now, that I might die quickly, that my soul might be gone to rest.

129. But before I had got thus far out of these my temptations, I did greatly long to see some ancient godly man's experience, who had writ some hundreds of years before I was born; for those who had writ in our days, I thought (but I desire them now to pardon me) that they had writ only that which others felt; or else had, through the strength of their wits and parts, studied to answer such objections as they perceived others were perplexed with, without going down themselves into the deep. Well, after many such longings in my mind, the God, in Whose hands are all our days and ways, did cast into my hand (one day) a book of **Martin Luther's**; it was his Comment on the **Galatians**; it also was so old, that it was ready to fall piece from piece if I did but turn it

over. Now I was pleased much that such an old book had fallen into my hand, the which when I had but a little way perused, I found my condition in his experience so largely and profoundly handled, as if his book had been written out of my heart. This made me marvel: for thus thought I, **This man could not know any thing of the state of Christians now**, **but must needs write and speak the experience of former days**.

130. Besides, he doth most gravely also in that book, debate of the rise of these temptations, namely, blasphemy, desperation, and the like; showing that the law of **Moses**, as well as the devil, death, and hell, hath a very great hand therein: the which, at first, was very strange to me; but considering and watching, I found it so indeed. But of particulars here, I intend nothing; only this methinks I must let fall before all men – I do prefer this book of **Martin Luther** upon the **Galatians** (excepting the Holy Bible) before all the

Grace Abounding to the Chief of Sinners

books that ever I had seen, as most fit for a wounded conscience.

131. And now I found, as I thought, that I loved Christ dearly: Oh! methought my soul cleaved unto Him, my affections cleaved unto Him; I felt love to Him as hot as fire; and now, as **Job** said, **I thought I should die in my nest**; but I did quickly find, that my great love was but little; and that I, who had, as I thought, such burning love to Jesus Christ, could let Him go again for a very trifle, – God can tell how to abase us, and can hide pride from man. Quickly after this my love was tried to purpose.

132. For after the Lord had, in this manner, thus graciously delivered me from this great and sore temptation, and had set me down so sweetly in the faith of His holy gospel, and had given me such strong consolation and blessed evidence from heaven, touching my interest in His love through Christ; the tempter came upon me again, and that with a more grievous and dreadful temptation

101

than before.

133. And that was, **To sell and part with this most blessed Christ, to exchange Him for the things of this life, for any thing**. The temptation lay upon me for the space of a year, and did follow me so continually, that I was not rid of it one day in a month: no, not sometimes one hour in many days together, unless when I was asleep.

134. And though, in my judgment, I was persuaded, that those who were once effectually in Christ (as I hoped, through His grace, I had seen myself) could never lose Him for ever; **The land shall not be sold for ever, for the land is mine**, saith God. Lev. xxv. 23. Yet it was a continual vexation to me, to think that I should have so much as one such thought within me against a Christ, a Jesus, that had done for me as He had done; and yet then I had almost none others, but such blasphemous ones.

135. But it was neither my dislike of the

thought, nor yet any desire and endeavour to resist, that in the least did shake or abate the continuation or force and strength thereof; for it did always, in almost whatever I thought, intermix itself therewith, in such sort, that I could neither eat my food, stoop for a pin, chop a stick, or cast mine eye to look on this or that, but still the temptation would come, **Sell Christ for this**, **or sell Christ for that**; **sell Him, sell Him**.

136. Sometimes it would run in my thoughts, not so little as a hundred times together, **Sell Him, sell Him, sell Him**: against which, I may say, for whole hours together, I have been forced to stand as continually leaning and forcing my spirit against it, lest haply, before I were aware, some wicked thought might arise in my heart, that might consent thereto; and sometimes the tempter would make me believe I had consented to it; but then I should be, as tortured upon a rack for whole days together.

137. This temptation did put me to such scares, lest I should at some times, I say, consent thereto, and be overcome therewith, that by the very force of my mind, in labouring to gainsay and resist this wickedness, my very body would be put into action or motion, by way of pushing or thrusting with my hands or elbows; still answering, as fast as the destroyer said, **Sell Him**; **I will not, I will not, I will not, I will not**; **no**, **not for thousands, thousands, thousands of worlds**: thus reckoning, lest I should, in the midst of these assaults, set too low a value on Him; even until I scarce well knew where I was, or how to be composed again.

138. At these seasons he would not let me eat my food at quiet; but, forsooth, when I was set at the table at my meat, I must go hence to pray; I must leave my food now, just now, so counterfeit holy also would this devil be. When I was thus tempted, I would say in myself, **Now I am at meat; let me make**

an end. No, said he, **you must do it now, or you will displease God, and despise Christ**. Wherefore I was much afflicted with these things; and because of the sinfulness of my nature (imagining that these were impulses from God), I should deny to do it, as if I denied God, and then should I be as guilty, because I did not obey a temptation of the devil, as if I had broken the law of God indeed.

139. But to be brief: one morning as I did lie in my bed, I was, as at other times, most fiercely assaulted with this temptation, **To sell and part with Christ**; the wicked suggestion still running in my mind, **Sell Him, sell Him, sell Him, sell Him, sell Him**, as fast as a man could speak: against which also, in my mind, as at other times, I answered, **No, no, not for thousands, thousands, thousands**, at least twenty times together: but at last, after much striving, even until I was almost out of breath, I felt this thought pass through my heart, **Let Him go, if He will**; and I thought

also, that I felt my heart freely consent thereto. Oh! the diligence of Satan! Oh! the desperateness of man's heart!

140. Now was the battle won, and down fell I as a bird that is shot from the top of a tree, into great guilt, and fearful despair. Thus getting out of my bed, I went moping into the field; but God knows, with as heavy a heart as mortal man, I think, could bear; where for the space of two hours, I was like a man bereft of life; and, as now, past all recovery, and bound over to eternal punishment.

141. And withal, that scripture did seize upon my soul: **Or profane persons as Esau, who for one morsel of meat, sold his birthright: for ye know, how that afterward, when he would have inherited the blessing, he was rejected; for he found no place of repentance, though he sought it carefully with tears**. Heb. xii. 16, 17.

142. Now was I as one bound, I felt myself shut up unto the judgment to come; nothing

now, for two years together, would abide with me, but damnation, and an expectation of damnation: I say, nothing now would abide with me but this, save some few moments for relief, as in the sequel you will see.

143. These words were to my soul, like fetters of brass to my legs, in the continual sound of which I went for several months together. But about ten or eleven o'clock on that day, as I was walking under an hedge (full of sorrow and guilt, God knows), and bemoaning myself for this hard hap, that such a thought should arise within me, suddenly this sentence rushed in upon me, **The blood of Christ remits all guilt**. At this I made a stand in my spirit: with that this word took hold upon me, **The blood of Jesus Christ His Son**, **cleanseth us from all sin**. 1 John i. 7.

144. Now I began to conceive peace in my soul, and methought I saw, as if the tempter did leer and steal away from me, as being ashamed of what he had done.

At the same time also I had my sin, and the blood of Christ, thus represented to me, That my sin, when compared to the blood of Christ, was no more to it, than this little clod or stone before me, is to this vast and wide field that here I see. This gave me good encouragement for the space of two or three hours; in which time also, methought, I saw, by faith, the Son of God, as suffering for my sins: but because it tarried not, I therefore sunk in my spirit, under exceeding guilt again.

145. But chiefly by the aforementioned scripture concerning **Esau's** selling of his birthright; for that scripture would lie all day long, all the week long, yea, all the year long in my mind, and hold me down, so that I could by no means lift up myself; for when I would strive to turn to this scripture or that, for relief, still that sentence would be sounding in me; **For ye know**, **how that afterwards**, **when he would have inherited the blessing**, **he found no**

place of repentance, though he sought it carefully with tears.

146. Sometimes, indeed, I should have a touch from that in Luke xxii. 31, **I have prayed for thee that thy faith fail not**; but it would not abide upon me; neither could I, indeed, when I considered my state, find ground to conceive in the least, that there should be the root of that grace in me, having sinned as I had done. Now was I tore and rent in an heavy case for many days together.

147. Then began I with sad and careful heart to consider of the nature and largeness of my sin, and to search into the word of God, if I could in any place espy a word of promise, or any encouraging sentence, by which I might take relief. Wherefore I began to consider that of Mark iii. 28: **All sins shall be forgiven unto the sons of men, and blasphemies wherewith soever they shall blaspheme**. Which place, methought at a blush, did contain a large and glorious promise for the pardon of high offences; but

considering the place more fully, I thought it was rather to be understood, as relating more chiefly to those who had, while in a natural estate, committed such things as there are mentioned; but not to me, who had not only received light and mercy, but that had both after, and also contrary to that, so slighted Christ as I had done.

148. I feared, therefore, that this wicked sin of mine, might be that sin unpardonable, of which He there thus speaketh. **But he that shall blaspheme against the Holy Ghost, hath never forgiveness, but is in danger of eternal damnation**. Mark iii. 29. And I did the rather give credit to this, because of that sentence in the Hebrews: **For you know how that afterwards, when he would have inherited the blessing, he was rejected; for he found no place of repentance, though he sought it carefully with tears**. And this stuck always with me.

149. And now was I both a burthen and a terror to myself; nor did I ever so know,

as now, what it was to be weary of my life, and yet afraid to die. Oh! how gladly now would I have been anybody but myself! anything but a man, and in any condition but my own! For there was nothing did pass more frequently over my mind, than that it was impossible for me to be forgiven my transgression, and to be saved from the wrath to come.

150. And now I began to call again time that was spent; wishing a thousand times twice told, that the day was yet to come when I should be tempted to such a sin; concluding with great indignation, both against my heart, and all assaults, how I would rather have been torn in pieces, than be found a consenter thereto. But alas! these thoughts, and wishings, and resolvings were now too late to help me; this thought had passed my heart, God hath let me go, and I am fallen. Oh! thought I, **that it were with me as in months past**, **as in the days when God preserved me**! Job xxix. 2.

151. Then again, being loth and unwilling to perish, I began to compare my sin with others to see if I could find that any of those that were saved, had done as I had done. So I considered **David's** adultery, and murder, and found them most heinous crimes; and those too committed after light and grace received: but yet by considering that his transgressions were only such as were against the law of **Moses**, from which the Lord Christ could, with the consent of His word, deliver him: but mine was against the gospel; yea, against the Mediator thereof; I had sold my Saviour.

152. Now again should I be as if racked upon the wheel, when I considered, that, besides the guilt that possessed me, I should be so void of grace, so bewitched. What, thought I, must it be no sin but this? Must it needs be the **great transgression**? Ps. xix. 13. Must **that wicked one** touch my soul? 1 John v. 18. Oh! what sting did I find in all these sentences?

153. What, thought I, is there but **one** sin that is unpardonable? but **one** sin that layeth the soul without the reach of God's mercy; and must I be guilty of **that**? must it needs be that? Is there but one **sin** among **so many** millions of sins, for which there is no forgiveness; and must I commit this? Oh! unhappy **sin**! Oh! unhappy **man**! These things would so break and confound my spirit, that I could not tell what to do; I thought at times, they would have broke my wits; and still, to aggravate my misery, that would run in my mind, **You know**, **how**, **that afterwards**, **when he would have inherited the blessing**, **he was rejected. Oh! no one knows the terrors of those days but myself**.

154. After this I began to consider of **Peter's** sin, which he committed in denying his Master: and indeed, this came nighest to mine of any that I could find, for he had denied his Saviour, as I, after light and mercy received; yea, and that too, after warning

given him. I also considered, that he did it both once and twice; and that, after time to consider betwixt. But though I put all these circumstances together, that, if possible I might find help, yet I considered again, that his was but **a denial of his Master**, but mine was, **a selling of my Saviour**. Wherefore I thought with myself, that I came nearer to **Judas**, than either to **David** or **Peter**.

155. Here again my torment would flame out and afflict me; yea, it would grind me, as it were to powder, to consider the preservation of God towards others, while I fell into the snare; for in my thus considering of other men's sins, and comparing them with mine own, I could evidently see, God preserved them, notwithstanding their wickedness, and would not let them, as He had let me, become a son of perdition.

156. But oh! how did my soul at this time prize the preservation that God did set about His people! Ah, how safely did I see them walk, whom God had hedged

in! They were within His care, protection, and special providence: though they were full as bad as I by nature; yet because He loved them, He would not suffer them to fall without the range of mercy: but as for me, I was gone, I had done it: He would not preserve me, nor keep me; but suffered me, because I was a reprobate, to fall as I had done. Now did those blessed places that speak of God's keeping His people, shine like the sun before me, though not to comfort me, yet to show me the blessed state and heritage of those whom the Lord had blessed.

157. Now I saw, that as God had His hand in all the providences and dispensations that overtook His elect; so He had His hand in all the temptations that they had to sin against Him; not to animate them to wickedness, but to choose their temptations and troubles for them; and also to leave them for a time, to such sins only that might not destroy, but humble them; as might not put them beyond,

but lay them in the way of the renewing His mercy. But oh! what love, what care, what kindness and mercy did I now see, mixing itself with the most severe and dreadful of all God's ways to His people! He would let **David**, **Hezekiah**, **Solomon**, **Peter**, and others, fall; but He would not let them fall into sin unpardonable, nor into hell for sin. Oh! thought I, these be the men that God hath loved; these be the men that God, though He chastiseth them, keeps them in safety by Him; and them whom He makes to abide under the shadow of the Almighty. But all these thoughts added sorrow, grief, and horror to me, as whatever I now thought on, it was killing to me. If I thought how God kept His own, that was killing to me; if I thought of how I was fallen myself, that was killing to me. As all things wrought together for the best, and to do good to them that were the called, according to His purpose, so I thought that all things wrought for my damage, and for my eternal overthrow.

158. Then again I began to compare my sin with the sin of **Judas**, that, if possible, I might find if mine differed from that, which in truth is unpardonable: and oh! thought I, if it should differ from it, though but the breadth of an hair, what a happy condition is my soul in! And by considering, I found that **Judas** did this intentionally, but mine was against my prayer and strivings: besides, his was committed with much deliberation, but mine in a fearful hurry, on a sudden: all this while I was tossed to and fro like the locusts, and driven from trouble to sorrow; hearing always the sound of **Esau's** fall in mine ears, and the dreadful consequences thereof.

159. Yet this consideration about **Judas's** sin was, for awhile, some little relief to me; for I saw I had not, as to the circumstances, transgressed so fully as he. But this was quickly gone again, for I thought with myself, there might be more ways than one to commit this unpardonable sin; also I thought there

might be degrees of that, as well as of other transgressions; wherefore, for aught I yet could perceive, this iniquity of mine might be such, as might never be passed by.

160. I was often now ashamed that I should be like such an ugly man as Judas: I thought also how loathsome I should be unto all the saints at the day of judgment: insomuch that now I could scarce see a good man, that I believed had a good conscience, but I should feel my heart tremble at him, while I was in his presence. Oh! now I saw a glory in walking with God, and what a mercy it was to have a good conscience before Him.

161. I was much about that time tempted to content myself by receiving some false opinion; as, that there should be no such thing as a day of judgment; that we should not rise again; and that sin was no such grievous thing: the tempter suggesting thus: **For if these things should indeed be true, yet to believe otherwise would**

yield you ease for the present. If you must perish, never torment yourself so much beforehand: **drive the thoughts of damning out of your mind**, **by possessing your mind with some such conclusions that** Atheists **and** Ranters **use to help themselves withal**.

162. But oh! when such thoughts have led through my heart, how, as it were, within a step, hath death and judgment been in my view! methought the judge stood at the door; I was as if it was come already; so that such things could have no entertainment. But methinks, I see by this, that Satan will use any means to keep the soul from Christ; he loveth not an awakened frame of spirit; security, blindness, darkness, and error, is the very kingdom and habitation of the wicked one.

163. I found it a hard work now to pray to God, because despair was swallowing me up; I thought I was as with a tempest driven away from God; for always when I cried to

God for mercy, this would come in, **'Tis too late, I am lost, God hath let me fall**; **not to my correction, but condemnation: my sin is unpardonable**; **and I know, concerning Esau, how that after he had sold his birthright, he would have received the blessing, but was rejected**. About this time I did light on that dreadful story of that miserable mortal Francis Spira; a book that was to my troubled spirit, as salt, when rubbed into a fresh wound: every sentence in that book, every groan of that man, with all the rest of his actions in his dolours, as his tears, his prayers, his gnashing of teeth, his wringing of hands, his twining and twisting, and languishing, and pining away under that mighty hand of God that was upon him, were as knives and daggers in my soul; especially that sentence of his was frightful to me, **Man knows the beginning of sin**? **but who bounds the issues thereof**? Then would the former sentence, as the conclusion of all, fall like an hot thunderbolt again upon my conscience; **For you know how that afterwards, when he would have inherited the blessing, he was rejected**; for he **found no place of repentance, though he sought it carefully with tears**.

164. Then should I be struck into a very great trembling, insomuch that at sometimes I could, for whole days together, feel my very body, as well as my mind, to shake and totter under the sense of this dreadful judgment of God, that should fall on those that have sinned that most fearful and unpardonable sin. I felt also such a clogging and heat at my stomach, by reason of this my terror, that I was, especially at some times, as if my breast-bone would split asunder; then I thought of that concerning Judas, who by **falling headlong, he burst asunder in the midst, and all his bowels gushed out**. Acts i. 18.

165. I feared also that this was the mark that the Lord did set on **Cain**, even continual fear and trembling, under the heavy load

of guilt that he had charged on him for the blood of his brother **Abel**. Thus did I wind, and twine, and shrink under the burthen that was upon me; which burthen also did so oppress me, that I could neither stand, nor go, nor lie, either at rest or quiet.

166. Yet that saying would sometimes come into my mind, **He hath received gifts for the rebellious**. Psalm lxviii. 18. The **rebellious**, thought I! why surely they are such as once were under subjection to their Prince; even those who after they have sworn subjection to His government, have taken up arms against Him; and this, thought I, is my very condition: I once loved Him, feared Him, served Him; but now I am a rebel; I have sold Him, I have said, **Let Him go**, **if He will**; but yet He has gifts for rebels; and then why not for me?

167. This sometimes I thought on, and should labour to take hold thereof, that some, though small refreshment, might have been conceived by me; but in this also I missed of

my desire; I was driven with force beyond it; I was like a man going to execution, even by **that** place where he would fain creep in and hide himself, but may not.

168. Again, after I had thus considered the sins of the **saints** in particular, and found **mine** went beyond them, then I began to think with myself, Set the case I should put **all theirs** together, and **mine alone** against them, might I not then find some encouragement? for if **mine**, though bigger than any one, yet should be but equal to all, then there is hopes; for that blood that hath virtue enough in it to wash away all theirs, had virtue enough in it to do away mine, though this one be full as big, if not bigger than all theirs. Here again, I should consider the sin of **David**, of **Solomon**, of **Manasseh**, of **Peter**, and the rest of the great offenders; and should also labour, what I might with fairness, to aggravate and heighten their sins by several circumstances.

169. I should think with myself that **David**

shed blood to cover his adultery, and that by the sword of the children of **Ammon**; a work that could not be done, but by continuance, deliberate contrivance, which was a great aggravation to his sin. But then this would turn upon me: Ah! but these were but sins against the law, from which there was a Jesus sent to save them; but yours is a sin against the Saviour, and who shall save you from that?

170. Then I thought on **Solomon**, and how he sinned in loving strange women, falling away to their idols, in building them temples, in doing this after light, in his old age, after great mercy received: but the same conclusion that cut me off in the former consideration, cut me off as to this; namely, that all those were but sins against the law, for which God had provided a remedy; **but I had sold my Saviour**, and there remained no more sacrifice for sin.

171. I would then add to these men's sins, the sins of **Manasseh**; how that he built

altars for idols in the house of the Lord; he also observed times, used enchantments, had to do with wizards, was a wizard, had his familiar spirits, burned his children in the fire in sacrifice to devils, and made the streets of **Jerusalem** run down with the blood of innocents. These, thought I, are great sins, sins of a bloody colour, but yet it would turn again upon me, **They are none of them of the nature of yours**; **you have parted with Jesus**, **you have sold your Saviour**.

172. This one consideration would always kill my heart, **my sin was point blank against my Saviour**; and that too, at that height, that I had in my heart said of Him, **Let Him go**, **if He will**. Oh! methought this sin was bigger than the sins of a country, of a kingdom, or of the whole world, **no** one pardonable; nor **all** of them together, was able to equal mine; mine out-went them every one.

173. Now I should find my mind to flee from God, as from the face of a dreadful judge, yet this was my torment, I could not escape

His hand: (**It is a fearful thing to fall into the hands of the living God**. Hebrew x.) But, blessed be His grace, that scripture, in these flying fits, would call, as running after me, **I have blotted out**, **as a thick cloud**, **thy transgressions**; **and as a cloud**, **thy sins**: **return unto Me**, **for I have redeemed thee**. Isaiah xliv. 22. This, I say, would come in upon my mind, when I was fleeing from the face of God; for I did flee from His face; that is, my mind and spirit fled before Him; by reason of His highness, I could not endure: then would the text cry, **Return unto Me**; it would cry aloud with a very great voice, **Return unto Me**, **for I have redeemed thee**. Indeed, this would make me make a little stop, and, as it were, look over my shoulder behind me, to see if I could discern that the God of grace did follow me with a pardon in His hand; but I could no sooner do that, but all would be clouded and darkened again by that sentence, **For you know, how that afterwards, when he would**

have inherited the blessing, **he found no place of repentance**, **though he sought it carefully with tears**. Wherefore I could not refrain, but fled, though at some times it cried, **Return**, **return**, as if it did hollow after me: but I feared to close in therewith, lest it should not come from God; for that other, as I said, was still sounding in my conscience, **For you know that afterwards**, **when he would have inherited the blessing**, **he was rejected**, **etc.**

174. Once as I was walking to and fro in a good man's shop, bemoaning of myself in my sad and doleful state, afflicting myself with self-abhorrence for this wicked and ungodly thought; lamenting also this hard hap of mine for that I should commit so great a sin, greatly fearing that I should not be pardoned; praying also in my heart, that if this sin of mine did differ from that against the Holy Ghost, the Lord would show it me. And being now ready to sink with fear, suddenly there was, as if there had rushed

in at the window, the noise of wind upon me, but very pleasant, and as if I heard a voice speaking, **Did'st thou ever refuse to be justified by the blood of Christ**? and withal, my whole life of profession past, was in a moment opened to me, wherein I was made to see, that designedly I had not: so my heart answered groaningly, **No**. Then fell, with power, that word of God upon me, **See that ye refuse not Him that speaketh**. Hebrew xii. 25. This made a strange seizure upon my spirit; it brought light with it, and commanded a silence in my heart, of all those tumultuous thoughts, that did before use, like masterless hell-hounds, to roar and bellow, and make an hideous noise within me. It showed me also that Jesus Christ had yet a word of grace and mercy for me, that He had not, as I had feared, quite forsaken and cast off my soul; yea, this was a kind of chide for my proneness to desperation; a kind of threatening of me, if I did not, notwithstanding my sins,

and the heinousness of them, venture my
salvation upon the Son of God. But as to my
determining about this strange dispensation,
what it was, I know not; or from whence it
came, I know not; I have not yet in twenty
years' time been able to make a judgment
of it; **I thought then what here I should
be loth to speak**. But verily that sudden
rushing wind was, as if an angel had come
upon me; but both it, and the salutation, I
will leave until the day of judgment: only
this I say, it commanded a great calm in my
soul; it persuaded me there might be hope:
it showed me, as I thought, what the sin
unpardonable was, and that my soul had
yet the blessed privilege to flee to Jesus
Christ for mercy. But I say, concerning this
dispensation; I know not yet what to say
unto it; which was also, in truth, the cause,
that at first I did not speak of it in the book;
I do now also leave it to be thought on by
men of sound judgment. I lay not the stress
of my salvation thereupon, but upon the

Lord Jesus, in the promise; yet seeing I am here unfolding of my secret things, I thought it might not be altogether inexpedient to let this also show itself, though I cannot now relate the matter as there I did experience it. This lasted in the savour of it for about three or four days, and then I began to mistrust, and to despair again.

175. Wherefore still my life hung in doubt before me, not knowing which way I should tip; only this I found my soul desire, even to cast itself at the foot of grace, by prayer and supplication. But oh! 'twas hard for me now, to have the face to pray to this Christ for mercy, against Whom I had thus most vilely sinned: 'twas hard work, I say, to offer to look Him in the face, against Whom I had so vilely sinned; and indeed, I have found it as difficult to come to God by prayer, after backsliding from Him, as to do any other thing. Oh! the shame that did now attend me! especially when I thought, I am now a-going to pray to Him

for mercy, that I had so lightly esteemed but a while before! I was ashamed; yea, even confounded, because this villany had been committed by me: but I saw that there was but one way with me; I must go to Him, and humble myself unto Him, and beg that He, of His wonderful mercy, would show pity to me, and have mercy upon my wretched sinful soul.

176. Which, when the tempter perceived, he strongly suggested to me, **That I ought not to pray to God, for prayer was not for any in my case; neither could it do me good, because I had rejected the Mediator, by Whom all prayers came with acceptance to God the Father; and without Whom, no prayer could come into His presence: wherefore now to pray, is but to add sin to sin; yea, now to pray, seeing God has cast you off, is the next way to anger and offend Him more than you ever did before.**

177. **For God** (saith he) **hath been weary of you for these several years already,**

because you are none of His; your bawlings in His ears, hath been no pleasant voice to Him; **and therefore He let you sin this sin, that you might be quite cut off; and will you pray still**? This the devil urged, and set forth that in **Numbers**, when **Moses** said to the children **of Israel, That because they would not go up to possess the land, when God would have them, therefore for ever after He did bar them out from thence, though they prayed they might with tears**. Numbers xiv. 36, 37, etc.

178. As it is said in another place, Exodus xxi. 14, **The man that sins presumptuously shall be taken from God's altar, that he may die**; even as **Joab** was by King **Solomon**, when he thought to find shelter there. 1 Kings ii. 27, 28, etc. These places did pinch me very sore; yet my case being desperate, I thought with myself, I can but die; and if it must be so, it shall once be said, **That such an one died at the foot of Christ in prayer**. This I did, but with great

difficulty, God doth know; and that because, together with this, still that saying about **Esau** would be set at my heart, even like a flaming sword, to keep the way of the tree of life, lest I should take thereof and live. Oh! who knows how hard a thing I found it, to come to God in prayer!

179. I did also desire the prayers of the people of God for me, but I feared that God would give them no heart to do it; yea I trembled in my soul to think, that some or other of them would shortly tell me, that God hath said those words to them, that He once did say to the prophet concerning the children of Israel, **Pray not for this people**, **for I have rejected them**. Jeremiah xi. 14. So, **Pray not for him**, **for I have rejected him**, yea, I thought that He had whispered this to some of them already, only they durst not tell me so; neither durst I ask them of it, for fear if it should be so, it would make me quite beside myself: **Man knows the beginning of sin (said Spira), but who bounds the issues**

thereof?

180. About this time I took an opportunity to break my mind to an ancient Christian, and told him all my case: I told him also, that I was afraid that I had sinned the sin against the Holy Ghost; and he told me, **He thought so too**. Here therefore I had but cold comfort; but talking a little more with him, I found him, though a good man, a stranger to much combat with the devil. Wherefore I went to God again, as well as I could, for mercy still.

181. Now also did the tempter begin to mock me in my misery, saying, **That seeing I had thus parted with the Lord Jesus, and provoked Him to displeasure, Who would have stood between my soul and the flame of devouring fire, there was now but one way**; **and that was**, to pray that God the Father would be a Mediator betwixt His Son and me; **that we might be reconciled again, and that I might have that blessed benefit in Him, that His blessed saints**

enjoyed.

182. Then did that scripture seize upon my soul, **He is of one mind**, **and who can turn Him**! Oh! I saw, it was as easy to persuade Him to make a new world, a new covenant, or a new Bible, besides that we have already, as to pray for such a thing. This was to persuade Him, that what He had done already was mere folly, and persuade Him to alter, yea, to disannul the whole way of salvation. And then would that saying rend my soul asunder; **Neither is there salvation in any other**; **for there is none other name under heaven given among men whereby we must be saved**. Acts iv. 12.

183. Now the most free, and full and gracious words of the gospel, were the greatest torment to me; yea, nothing so afflicted me, as the thoughts of Jesus Christ, the remembrance of a Saviour; because I had cast Him off, brought forth the villany of my sin, and my loss by it, to

mind; nothing did twinge my conscience like this: every time that I thought of the Lord Jesus, of His grace, love, goodness, kindness, gentleness, meekness, death, blood, promises, and blessed exhortations, comforts, and consolations, it went to my soul like a sword; for still unto these my considerations of the Lord Jesus, these thoughts would make place for themselves in my heart: **Aye, this is the Jesus, the loving Saviour, the Son of God, Whom you have parted with, Whom you have slighted, despised, and abused. This is the only Saviour, the only Redeemer, the only One that could so love sinners, as to wash them from their sins in His own most precious blood; but you have no part nor lot in this Jesus: you have put Him from you; you have said in your heart,** Let Him go, if He will. **Now, therefore, you are severed from Him; you have severed yourself from Him: behold then His goodness, but yourself**

to be no partaker of it. Oh! thought I, what have I lost, what have I parted with! What has disinherited my poor soul! Oh! 'tis sad to be destroyed by the grace and mercy of God; to have the Lamb, the Saviour, turn lion and destroyer. Rev. vi. I also trembled, as I have said, at the sight of the saints of God, especially at those that greatly loved Him, and that made it their business to walk continually with Him in this world; for they did, both in their words, their carriages, and all their expressions of tenderness and fear to sin against their precious Saviour, condemn, lay guilt upon, and also add continual affliction and shame upon my soul. **The dread of them was upon me, and I trembled at God's Samuels**. 1 Sam. xvi. 4.

184. Now also the tempter began afresh to mock my soul another way, saying, **That Christ indeed did pity my case**, **and was sorry for my loss**; **but forasmuch as I had sinned and transgressed as I had done**,

He could by no means help me, nor save me from what I feared: for my sin was not of the nature of theirs, for Whom He bled and died; neither was it counted with those that were laid to His charge, when He hanged on a tree: therefore, unless He should come down from heaven, and die anew for this sin, though indeed He did greatly pity me, yet I could have no benefit of Him. These things may seem ridiculous to others, even as ridiculous as they were in themselves, but to me they were most tormenting cogitations: every one of them augmented my misery, that Jesus Christ should have so much love as to pity me, when yet He could not help me; nor did I think that the reason why He could not help me, was, because His merits were weak, or His grace and salvation spent on others already, but because His faithfulness to His threatening, would not let Him extend His mercy to me. Besides, I thought, as I have already hinted, that my sin was not within the bounds of that pardon, that was wrapped up in a promise; and if not, then I knew assuredly, that it was more easy for heaven and earth to pass away, than for me to have eternal life. So that the ground of all these fears of mine did arise from a steadfast belief I had of the stability of the holy word of God, and also from my being misinformed of the nature of my sin.

185. But oh! how this would add to my affliction, to conceit that I should be guilty of such a sin, for which He did not die. These thoughts would so confound me, and imprison me, and tie me up from faith, that I knew not what to do. But oh! thought I, that He would come down again! Oh! that the work of man's redemption was yet to be done by Christ! how would I pray Him and entreat Him to count and reckon this sin among the rest for which He died! But this scripture would strike me down as dead; **Christ being raised from the dead**, **dieth no more**; **death hath no more dominion**

over Him. Rom. vi. 9.

186. Thus, by the strange and unusual assaults of the tempter, my soul was like a broken vessel, driven as with the winds, and tossed sometimes headlong into despair; sometimes upon the covenant of works, and sometimes to wish that the new covenant, and the conditions thereof, might so far forth, as I thought myself concerned, be turned another way, and changed, **But in all these, I was as those that jostle against the rocks**; **more broken, scattered and rent**. Oh! the un-thought-of imaginations, frights, fears, and terrors, that are affected by a thorough application of guilt yielding to desperation! **This is the man that hath his dwelling among the tombs with the dead**; **that is always crying out**, **and cutting himself with stones**. Mark v. 1, 2, 3. But, I say, all in vain; desperation will not comfort him, the old covenant will not save him: nay, heaven and earth shall pass away, before one jot

or tittle of the word and law of grace will fail or be removed. This I saw, this I felt, and under this I groaned; yet this advantage I got thereby, namely, a farther confirmation of the certainty of the way of salvation; and that the scriptures were the word of God. Oh! I cannot now express what then I saw and felt of the steadiness of Jesus Christ, the rock of man's salvation: What was done, could not be undone, added to, nor altered. I saw, indeed, that sin might drive the soul beyond Christ, even the sin which is unpardonable; but woe to him that was so driven, for the word would shut him out.

187. Thus I was always sinking, whatever I did think or do. So one day I walked to a neighbouring town, and sate down upon a settle in the street, and fell into a very deep pause about the most fearful state my sin had brought me to; and after long musing, I lifted up I sat my head, but methought I saw, as if the sun that shineth in the heavens did grudge to give light; and as if the very

stones in the street, and tiles upon the houses, did bend themselves against me. Methought that they all combined together to banish me out of the world. I was abhorred of them, and unfit to dwell among them, or be partaker of their benefits, because I had sinned against the Saviour. O how happy now was every creature over I was! For they stood fast, and kept their station, but I was gone and lost.

188. Then breaking out in the bitterness of my soul, I said to myself with a grievous sigh, **How can God comfort such a wretch**! I had no sooner said it, but this returned upon me, as an echo doth answer a voice: **This sin is not unto death**. At which I was, as if I had been raised out of the grave, and cried out again, **Lord, how couldst Thou find out such a word as this**! For I was filled with admiration at the fitness, and at the unexpectedness of the sentence; the fitness of the word, the rightness of the timing of it; the power, and sweetness, and light, and

glory that came with it also, were marvellous to me to find: I was now, for the time, out of doubt, as to that about which I was so much in doubt before; my fears before **were**, that my sin was not pardonable, and so that I had no right to pray, to repent, etc., or that, if I did, it would be of no advantage or profit to me. But now, thought I, if **this sin** is not unto death, then it is pardonable; therefore from this I have encouragement to come to God by Christ for mercy, to consider the promise of forgiveness, as that which stands with open arms to receive me as well as others. This therefore was a great easement to my mind, to wit, that my sin was pardonable, that it was not the sin unto death (1 John v. 16, 17). None but those that know what my trouble (by their own experience) was, can tell what relief came to my soul by this consideration: it was a release to me from my former bonds, and a shelter from the former storm: I seemed now to stand upon the same ground with other sinners, and to have as good right to the word and prayer as any of they.

189. Now I say, I was in hopes that my sin was not unpardonable, but that there might be hopes for me to obtain forgiveness. But oh! how Satan did now lay about him for to bring me down again! But he could by no means do it, neither this day, nor the most part of the next, for this good sentence stood like a mill-post at my back: yet towards the evening of the next day, I felt this word begin to leave me, and to withdraw its supportation from me, and so I returned to my old fears again, but with a great deal of grudging and peevishness, for I feared the sorrow of despair; nor could my faith now long retain this word.

190. But the next day at evening, being under many fears, I went to seek the Lord, and as I prayed, I cried, and my soul cried to Him in these words, with strong cries: **O Lord, I beseech Thee, show me that Thou hast loved me with everlasting**

love. Jer. xxxi. 3. I had no sooner said it, but with sweetness this returned upon me, as an echo, or sounding again, **I have loved thee with an everlasting love**. Now I went to bed in quiet; also when I awakened the next morning, it was fresh upon my soul; and I believed it.

191. But yet the tempter left me not; for it could not be so little as an hundred times, that he that day did labour to then break my peace. Oh! the combats and conflicts that I did then meet with; as I strove to hold by this word, that of **Esau** would fly in my face like lightning: I should be sometimes up and down twenty times in an hour; yet God did bear me up, and keep my heart upon this word; from which I had also, for several days together, very much sweetness, and comfortable hopes of pardon: for thus it was made out unto me, **I loved thee whilst thou wast committing this sin, I loved thee before, I love thee still, and I will love thee for ever**.

192. Yet I saw my sin most barbarous, and a filthy crime, and could not but conclude, and that with great shame and astonishment, that I had horribly abused the holy Son of God: wherefore I felt my soul greatly to love and pity Him, and my bowels to yearn towards Him; for I saw He was still my friend, and did reward me good for evil; yea, the love and affection that then did burn within to my Lord and Saviour Jesus Christ, did work at this time such a strong and hot desire of revengement upon myself for the abuse I had done unto Him, that to speak as I then thought, had I had a thousand gallons of blood within my veins, I could freely then have spilt it all, at the command and feet of this my Lord and Saviour.

193. And as I was thus in musing, and in my studies, considering how to love the Lord, and to express my love to Him, that saying came in upon me, **If Thou, Lord, shouldst mark iniquities, O Lord, who should stand? But there is forgiveness with Thee, that Thou**

mayest be feared. Psalm cxxx. 3, 4. These were good words to me, especially the latter part thereof; to wit, that there is forgiveness with the Lord, that He might be feared; that is, as then I understood it, that He might be loved, and had in reverence; for it was thus made out to me, **That the great God did set so high an esteem upon the love of His poor creatures, that rather than He would go without their love, He would pardon their transgressions**.

194. And now was that word fulfilled on me, and I was also refreshed by it; **That thou mayest remember and be confounded, and never open thy mouth any more, because of thy shame, when I am pacified toward thee for all that thou hast done, saith the Lord God**. Ezek. xvi. 63. Thus was my soul at this time (and as I then did think for ever) set at liberty from being afflicted with my former guilt and amazement.

195. But before many weeks were gone, I began to despond again, fearing, lest,

notwithstanding all that I had enjoyed, that I might be deceived and destroyed at the last; for this consideration came strong into my mind, **That whatever comfort and peace I thought I might have from the word of the promise of life**, yet unless there could be found in my refreshment, a concurrence and agreement in the scriptures, let me think what I will thereof, and hold it never so fast, I should find no such thing at the end; And the scripture cannot be broken. John x. 35.

196. Now began my heart again to ache, and fear I might meet with a disappointment at last. Wherefore I began with all seriousness to examine my former comfort, and to consider whether one that had sinned as I had done, might with confidence trust upon the faithfulness of God, laid down in those words, by which I had been comforted, and on which I had leaned myself: but now were brought those sayings to my mind. **For it is impossible for those who were**

once enlightened, and have tasted of the heavenly gift, and were made partakers of the Holy Ghost, and have tasted the good word of God, and the powers of the world to come, if they shall fall away, to renew them again unto repentance. Heb. vi. 4–6. **For, if we sin wilfully, after we have received the knowledge of the truth, there remains no more sacrifice for sin, but a certain fearful looking for of judgment, and fiery indignation, which shall devour the adversaries.** Heb. x. 26, 27. **As Esau, who for one morsel of meat, sold his birthright. For ye know how that afterward, when he would have inherited the blessing, he was rejected; for he found no place of repentance, though he sought it carefully with tears.** Heb. xii. 16, 17.

197. Now was the word of the gospel forced from my soul; so that no promise or encouragement was to be found in the Bible for me: and now would that saying work upon

my spirit to afflict me, **Rejoice not**, **O Israel**, **for joy**, **as other people**. Hos. ix. 1. For I saw indeed, there was cause of rejoicing for those that held to Jesus; but for me, I had cut myself off by my transgressions, and left myself neither foot-hold, or hand-hold, among all the stays and props in the precious word of life.

198. And truly, I did now feel myself to sink into a gulph, as an house whose foundation is destroyed; I did liken myself in this condition, unto the case of some child that was fallen into a mill-pit, who though it could make some shift to scramble and sprawl in the water, yet because it could find neither hold for hand nor foot, therefore at last it must die in that condition. So soon as this fresh assault had fastened on my soul, that scripture came into my heart, This **for many days**. Dan. x. 14. And indeed I found it was so; for I could not be delivered, nor brought to peace again, until well nigh two years and a half were completely finished. Wherefore these

words, though in themselves, they tended to discouragement, yet to me, who feared this condition would be eternal, they were at some times as an help and refreshment to me.

199. For, thought I, **many days** are not for ever, **many days** will have an end; therefore seeing I was to be afflicted not a few but **many days**, yet I was glad it was but **for many days**. Thus, I say, I would recall myself sometimes, and give myself an help, for as soon as ever the words came into my mind, at first, I knew my trouble would be long, yet this would be but sometimes; for I could not always think on this, nor ever be helped by it, though I did.

200. Now while the scriptures lay before me, and laid sin anew at my door, that saying, in Luke xviii. 1, with others, did encourage me to prayer: then the tempter laid again at me very sore, suggesting, **That neither the mercy of God**, **nor yet the blood of Christ**, **did at all concern me, nor could they help**

me for my sin; therefore it was but in vain to pray. Yet, thought I, **I will pray. But**, said the tempter, **your sin is unpardonable**. Well, said I, **I will pray**. 'Tis to no boot, said he. Yet said I, **I will pray**. So I went to prayer to God; and while I was at prayer, I uttered words to this effect: **Lord, Satan tells me, that neither Thy mercy, nor Christ's blood, is sufficient to save my soul: Lord, shall I honour Thee most, by believing Thou wilt, and canst? or him, by believing Thou neither wilt not nor canst? Lord, I would fain honour Thee, by believing Thou wilt and canst.**

201. And as I was thus before the Lord, that scripture fastened on my heart (O man, great is thy faith), Matt. xv. 28, even as if one had clapped me on the back, as I was on my knees before God: yet I was not able to believe this, that this was a prayer of faith, till almost six months after; for I could not think that I had faith, or that there should be a word for me to act faith on;

therefore I should still be, as sticking in the jaws of desperation, and went mourning up and down in a sad condition.

202. There was nothing now that I longed for more than to be put out of doubt, as to this thing in question, and as I was vehemently desiring to know, if there was indeed hope for me, these words came rolling into my mind, **Will the Lord cast off for ever**? **and will He be favourable no more**? **Is His mercy clean gone for ever**? **Doth His promise fail for evermore**? **Hath God forgotten to be gracious**? **Hath He in anger shut up His tender mercies**? Ps. lxxvii. 7–9. And all the while they run in my mind, methought I had still this as the answer, '**Tis a question whether He hath or no**: **it may be He hath not**. Yea, the interrogatory seemed to me to carry in it a sure affirmation that indeed He had not, nor would so cast off, but would be favourable: that His promise doth not fail, and that He had not forgotten to be gracious, nor would in anger shut up tender mercy.

Something also there was upon my heart at the same time, which I cannot now call to mind, which, with this text, did sweeten my heart, and make me conclude, that His mercy might not be quite gone, nor clean gone for ever.

203. At another time I remembered, I was again much under this question, **Whether the blood of Christ was sufficient to save my soul**? in which doubt I continued from morning, till about seven or eight at night: and at last, when I was, as it were, quite worn out with fear, lest it should not lay hold on me, these words did sound suddenly within my heart: **He is able**. But methought, this word **able**, was spoke loud unto me; it showed a **great word**, it seemed to be writ in **great letters**, and gave such a jostle to my fear and doubt (I mean for the time it tarried with me, which was about a day) as I never had from that, all my life, either before or after. Heb. vii. 25.

204. But one morning as I was again at

154

prayer, and trembling under the fear of this, **That no word of God could help me**, that piece of a sentence darted in upon me, **My grace is sufficient**. At this, methought I felt some stay, as if there might be hopes. But, oh! how good a thing it is for God to send His word! for, about a fortnight before, I was looking on this very place, and then I thought it could not come near my soul with comfort, therefore I threw down my book in a pet: then I thought it was not large enough for me; no, not large enough; but now it was as if it had arms of grace so wide, that it could not only enclose me, but many more such as I besides.

205. By these words I was sustained, yet not without exceeding conflicts, for the space of seven or eight weeks; for my peace would be in it, and out, sometimes twenty times a day; comfort now, and trouble presently; peace now, and before I could go a furlong, as full of fear and guilt as ever heart could hold. And this was not only

now and then, but my whole seven weeks' experience: for this about **the sufficiency of grace**, and **that** of **Esau's** parting with his birthright, would be like a pair of scales within my mind; sometimes one end would be uppermost, and sometimes again the other; according to which would be my peace or trouble.

206. Therefore I did still pray to God, that He would come in with this scripture more fully on my heart; to wit, that He would help me to apply the whole sentence, for as yet I could not: that He gave, that I gathered; but farther I could not go, for as yet it only helped me to hope there might be mercy for me; **My grace is sufficient**: And though it came no farther, it answered my former question, to wit, That there was hope; yet because **for thee** was left out, I was not contented, but prayed to God for that also. Wherefore, one day, when I was in a meeting of God's people, full of sadness and terror; for my fears again were strong upon me; and, as

I was now thinking, my soul was never the better, but my case most sad and fearful, these words did with great power suddenly break in upon me; **My grace is sufficient for thee**, **My grace is sufficient for thee**, **My grace is sufficient for thee**, three times together: And oh! methought that every word was a mighty word unto me; as **My**, and **grace**, and **sufficient**, and **for thee**; they were then, and sometimes are still, far bigger than others be.

207. At which time my understanding was so enlightened, that I was as though I had seen the Lord Jesus look down from heaven, through the tiles upon me, and direct these words unto me. This sent me mourning home; it broke my heart, and filled me full of joy, and laid me low as the dust; only it stayed not long with me, I mean in this glory and refreshing comfort; yet it continued with me for several weeks, and did encourage me to hope: but as soon as that powerful operation of it was taken from my heart, that other, about **Esau**,

returned upon me as before: so my soul did hang as in a pair of scales again, sometimes up, and sometimes down; now in peace, and anon again in terror.

208. Thus I went on for many weeks, sometimes comforted, and sometimes tormented; and especially at sometimes my torment would be very sore, for all those scriptures forenamed in the **Hebrews**, would be set before me, as the only sentences that would keep me out of heaven. Then again I would begin to repent that ever that thought went through me; I would also think thus with myself: **Why, how many scriptures are there against me? There are but three or four; And cannot God miss them, and save me for all them?** Sometimes again I would think, **Oh! if it were not for these three or four words, now how might I be comforted!** And I could hardly forbear at some times, to wish them out of the book.

209. Then methought I should see as if

both **Peter** and **Paul**, and **John**, and all the writers, did look with scorn upon me, and hold me in derision; and as if they had said unto me, **All our words are truth**, **one of as much force as another**: **it is not we that have cut you of**, **but you have cast away yourself**. **There is none of our sentences that you must take hold upon**, **but these and such as these**; **it is impossible**, Heb. vi.; **there remains no more sacrifice for sin**, Heb. x. **And it had been better for them not to have known the will of God**, **than after they had known it**, **to turn from the holy commandment delivered unto them**, 2 Peter ii. 21. **For the Scriptures cannot be broken**. John x. 35.

210. These, as the elders of the city of refuge, I saw, were to be judges both of my case and me, while I stood with the **avenger** of blood at my heels, trembling at their gate for deliverance; also with a thousand fears and mistrusts, I doubted that they would shut me out for ever. Joshua xx. 3. 4.

211. Thus I was confounded, not knowing what to do, or how to be satisfied in this question, **Whether the scriptures could agree in the salvation of my soul**? I quaked at the apostles; I knew their words were true, and that they must stand for ever.

212. And I remember one day, as I was in divers frames of spirit, and considering that these frames were according to the nature of several scriptures that came in upon my mind; if this of grace, then was I quiet; but of that of **Esau**, then tormented. Lord, thought I, **if both these scriptures should meet in my heart at once, I wonder which of them would get the better of me**. So methought I had a longing mind that they might come both together upon me; yea, I desired of God they might.

213. Well, about two or three days after, so they did indeed; they bolted both upon me at a time, and did work and struggle strangely in me for a while; at last that about **Esau's** birthright began to wax weak, and withdraw,

and vanish; and this, about the sufficiency of grace prevailed with peace and joy. And as I was in a muse about this thing, that scripture came in upon me, **Mercy rejoiceth against judgment**. James ii. 13.

214. This was a wonderment to me; yet truly, I am apt to think it was of God; for the word of the law and wrath, must give place to the word of life and grace; because, though the word of condemnation be glorious, yet the word of life and salvation doth far exceed in glory. 2 Cor. iii. 8–11. **Mark** ix. 5–7. **John** vi. 37. Also that **Moses** and **Elias** must both vanish, and leave Christ and His saints alone.

215. This scripture also did now most sweetly visit my soul; **And him that cometh to Me, I will in no wise cast out**. Oh! the comfort that I had from this word, **in no wise**! As who should say, **By no means**, **for nothing whatever he hath done**. But Satan would greatly labour to pull this promise from me, telling of me, **That Christ did not mean me and such**

as I, but sinners of a lower rank, that had not done as I had done. But I would answer him again, **Satan, here is in these words no such exception; but him that comes, him, any him: him that cometh to Me I will in no wise cast out**. And this I well remember still, that of all the slights that Satan used to take this scripture from me, yet he never did so much as put this question, **But do you come aright**? And I have thought the reason was, because he thought I knew full well what coming aright was; for I saw that to come aright, was to come as I was, a vile and ungodly sinner, and to cast myself at the feet of mercy, condemning myself for sin. If ever Satan and I did strive for any word of God in all my life, it was for this good word of Christ; he at one end, and I at the other: Oh! what work did we make! It was for this in **John**, I say, that we did so tug and strive, he pulled, and I pulled; but God be praised, I got the better of him; I got some sweetness from it.

216. But notwithstanding all these helps, and blessed words of grace, yet that of **Esau's** selling of his birthright, would still at times distress my conscience: for though I had been most sweetly comforted, and that but just before, yet when that came into my mind, 'twould make me fear again: I could not be quite rid thereof, 'twould every day be with me: wherefore now I went another way to work, even to consider the nature of this blasphemous thought, I mean, if I should take the words at the largest, and give them their own natural force and scope, even every word therein: so when I had thus considered, I found, that if they were fairly taken, they would amount to this; **That I had freely left the Lord Jesus Christ to His choice, whether He would be my Saviour or no**; for the wicked words were these, **Let Him go, if He will**. Then that scripture gave me hope, **I will never leave thee, nor forsake thee**. Heb. xiii. 5. 'O Lord,' said I, **but I have**

left Thee. Then it answered again, **But I will not leave thee**. For this I thanked God also.

217. Yet I was grievous afraid He should, and found it exceeding hard to trust Him, seeing I had so offended Him: I could have been exceeding glad that this thought had never befallen; for then I thought I could with more ease and freedom in abundance, have leaned on His grace. I saw it was with me, as it was with **Joseph's** brethren; the guilt of their own wickedness did often fill them with fears that their brother would at last despise them. Gen. l. 15, 16, etc.

218. Yet above all the scriptures that I yet did meet with that in **Joshua** xx. was the greatest comfort to me, which speaks of the slayer that was to flee for refuge: **And if the avenger of blood pursue the slayer**, then saith **Moses, they that are the elders of the city of refuge shall not deliver him into his hands, because he smote his neighbour unwittingly and hated him not aforetime**. Oh! blessed be God for this

word: I was convinced that I was the slayer; and that the avenger of blood pursued me, I felt with great terror; only now it remained that I inquire whether I have right to enter the city of refuge: so I found, that he must not, **who lay in wait to shed blood**: It was not the wilful **murderer**, but he who **unwittingly** did it, he who did it unawares; not out of spite, or grudge, or malice, he that shed it unwittingly: even he who did not **hate his neighbour before**. Wherefore,

219. I thought verily I was the man that must enter, because I had smitten my neighbour **unwittingly**, **and hated Him not aforetime**. I hated Him not aforetime; no, I prayed unto Him, was tender of sinning against Him; yea, and against this wicked temptation I had strove for a twelvemonth before; yea, and also when it did pass through my heart, it did in spite of my teeth: wherefore I thought I had a right to enter this city, and the elders, which are the **apostles**, were not to deliver me up.

This therefore was great comfort to me, and gave me much ground of hope.

220. Yet being very critical, for my smart had made me that I knew not what ground was sure enough to bear me, I had one question that my soul did much desire to be resolved about; and that was, **Whether it be possible for any soul that hath sinned the unpardonable sin, yet after that to receive, though but the least, true spiritual comfort from God though Christ**? The which after I had much considered, I found the answer was, No, they could not; and that for these reasons: –

221. **First**, Because those that have sinned that sin, they are debarred a share in the blood of Christ; and being shut out of that, they must needs be void of the least ground of hope, and so of spiritual comfort; **For to such there remains no more sacrifice for sin**. Heb. x. 26, 27. **Secondly**, Because they are denied a share in the promise of life: **It shall never**

be forgiven him neither in this world, neither in the world to come. Matt. xii. 32. **Thirdly**, The Son of God excludes them also from a share in His blessed intercession, being for ever ashamed to own them, both before His holy Father, and the blessed angels in heaven. Mark viii.

222. When I had with much deliberation considered of this matter, and could not but conclude that the Lord had comforted me, and that too after this my wicked sin: then methought I durst venture to come nigh unto those most fearful and terrible scriptures, with which all this while I had been so greatly affrighted, and on which indeed, before I durst scarce cast mine eye (yea, had much ado an hundred times, to forbear wishing them out of the Bible), for I thought they would destroy me; but now, I say, I began to take some measure of encouragement, to come close to them to read them, and consider them, and to weigh their scope and tendency.

223. The which when I began to do, I found their visage changed: for they looked not so grimly, as before I thought they did: and first I came to the sixth of the **Hebrews**, yet trembling for fear it should strike me; which when I had considered, I found that the falling there intended, was a falling **quite away**; that is as I conceived, a falling from and absolute denying of the gospel, of remission of sins by Jesus Christ; for, from them the apostle begins his argument, verses 1, 2, 3, 4. **Secondly**, I found that this falling away, must be openly, even in the view of the world, even so as **to put Christ to an open shame**. **Thirdly**, I found those he there intended, were for ever shut up of God, both in blindness, hardness, and impenitency: **It is impossible they should be renewed again unto repentance**. By all these particulars, I found to God's everlasting praise, my sin was not the sin in this place intended.

First, I confessed I was fallen, but not fallen away; that is, from the profession of faith in

Jesus unto eternal life.

Secondly, I confessed that I had put Jesus Christ to **shame** by my sin, but not to open **shame**; I did not deny Him before men, nor condemn Him as a fruitless One before the world.

Thirdly, Nor did I find that God had shut me up, or denied me to come (though I found it hard work indeed to come) to Him by sorrow and repentance: blessed be God for unsearchable grace!

224. Then I considered that in the 10th chapter of the **Hebrews**, and found that the **wilful sin** there mentioned, is not every wilful sin, but that which doth throw off Christ, and then His commandments too. **Secondly**, That must be done also openly, before two or three witnesses, to answer that of the law, **verse** 28. **Thirdly**, This sin cannot be committed, but with great despite done to the Spirit of Grace; despising both the dissuasions from that sin, and the persuasions to the contrary.

But the Lord knows, though this my sin was devilish, yet it did not amount to these.

225. And as touching that in the 12th of the **Hebrews**, about **Esau's** selling of his birthright; though this was that which killed me, and stood like a spear against me, yet now I did consider, **First**, that his was not a hasty thought against the continual labour of his mind, but a thought consented to, and put in practice likewise, and that after some deliberation, Gen. xxv. **Secondly**, It was a public and open action, even before his brother, if not before many more; this made his sin of a far more heinous nature than otherwise it would have been. **Thirdly**, He continued to slight his birthright: **He did eat and drink**, **and went his way**: thus Esau **despised his birthright**, yea, twenty years after he was found to despise it still. And Esau said, **I have enough**, **my brother**, **keep that thou hast unto thyself**. Gen. xxxiii. 9.

226. Now as touching this, **that Esau sought**

a place of repentance; thus I thought: **First**, This was not for the **birthright**, but **the blessing**: this is clear from the apostle, and is distinguished by Esau himself; **He took away my birthright** (that is, formerly); **and behold now he hath taken away my blessing**. Gen. xxvii. 36. **Secondly**, Now, this being thus considered, I came again to the apostle, to see what might be the mind of God, in a New-Testament style and sense concerning **Esau's** sin; and so far as I could conceive, this was the mind of God, **that the birthright** signified **regeneration**, and the **blessing**, the **eternal inheritance**; for so the apostle seems to hint. **Lest there be any profane person**, **as** Esau, **who for one morsel of meat sold his birthright**; as if he should say, That shall cast off all those blessed beginnings of God, that at present are upon him, in order to a new-birth; lest they become as **Esau**, even be rejected **afterwards**, when they would inherit the blessing.

227. For many there are, who, in the day of grace and mercy, despise those things which are indeed the birthright to heaven, who yet when the deciding day appears, will cry as lord as **Esau, Lord, Lord, open to us**; but then, as **Isaac** would not repent, no more will God the Father, but will say, **I have blessed these, yea**, and **they shall be blessed**; but as for you, **Depart, you are the workers of iniquity**. Gen. xxvii. 32; Luke xiii. 25–27.

228. When I had thus considered these scriptures, and found that thus to understand them, was not against, but according to other scriptures; this still added further to my encouragement and comfort, and also gave a great blow to that objection, to wit, **That the scriptures could not agree in the salvation of my soul**. And now remained only the hinder part of the tempest, for the thunder was gone beyond me, only some drops did still remain, that now and then would fall upon me; but because my

former frights and anguish were very sore and deep, therefore it oft befall me still, as it befalleth those that have been scared with fire. I thought every voice was, **Fire! fire**! Every little touch would hurt my tender conscience.

229. But one day, as I was passing in the field, and that too with some dashes on my conscience, fearing lest yet all was not right, suddenly this sentence fell upon my soul, **Thy righteousness is in heaven**; and methought withal, I saw with the eyes of my soul, Jesus Christ at God's right hand: there, I say, was my righteousness; so that wherever I was, or whatever I was doing, God could not say of me, **He wants My righteousness**; for that was just before Him. I also saw moreover, that it was not my good frame of heart that made my righteousness better, nor yet my bad frame that made my righteousness worse; for my righteousness was Jesus Christ Himself, **The same yesterday**, **to-day**, **and for**

ever. Heb. xiii. 8.

230. Now did my chains fall off my legs indeed; I was loosed from my afflictions and irons; my temptations also fled away; so that from that time those dreadful scriptures of God left off to trouble me: now went I also home rejoicing, for the grace and love of God; so when I came home, I looked to see if I could find that sentence; **Thy righteousness is in heaven**, but could not find such a saying; wherefore my heart began to sink again, only that was brought to my remembrance, 1 Cor. i. 30, **Christ Jesus**, **who of God is made unto us wisdom**, **and righteousness**, **and sanctification**, **and redemption**; by this word I saw the other sentence true.

231. For by this scripture I saw that the Man Christ Jesus, as He is distinct from us, as touching His bodily presence, so He is our righteousness and sanctification before God. Here therefore I lived, for some time, very sweetly at peace with God through

Christ; Oh! methought, Christ! Christ! there was nothing but Christ that was before my eyes: I was not now (only) for looking upon this and the other benefits of Christ apart, as of His blood, burial, or resurrection, but considering Him as a whole Christ! as He in whom all these, and all His other virtues, relations, offices and operations met together, and that He sat on the right hand of God in heaven.

232. 'Twas glorious to me to see His exaltation, and the worth and prevalency of all His benefits, and that because now I could look from myself to Him and should reckon, that all those graces of God that now were green on me, were yet but like those cracked groats and fourpence-halfpennies that rich men carry in their purses, when their gold is in their trunks at home: Oh! I saw my gold was in my trunk at home! In Christ my Lord and Saviour. Now Christ was all; all my wisdom, all my righteousness, all my sanctification, and all my redemption.

233. Further, the Lord did also lead me into the mystery of union with the Son of God; that I was joined to Him, that I was flesh of His flesh, and bone of His bone; and now was that word sweet to me in Eph. v. 30. By this also was my faith in Him, as my righteousness, the more confirmed in me; for if He and I were one, then His righteousness was mine, His merits mine, His victory also mine. Now could I see myself in heaven and earth at once: in heaven by my Christ, by my head, by my righteousness and life, though on earth by my body or person.

234. Now I saw Christ Jesus was looked upon of God; and should also be looked upon by us, as that common or public person, in whom all the whole body of His elect are always to be considered and reckoned; that we fulfilled the law by Him, died by Him, rose from the dead by Him, got the victory over sin, death, the devil, and hell, by Him; when He died, we died,

and so of His resurrection. **Thy dead men shall live, together with My dead body shall they arise**, saith He. Isa. xxvi. 19. And again, **after two days He will revive us, and the third day He will raise us up, and we shall live in His sight**. Hosea vi. 2. Which is now fulfilled by the sitting down of the Son of Man on the right hand of the Majesty in the heavens; according to that to the **Ephesians, And hath raised us up together, and made us sit together in heavenly places in Christ Jesus**. Eph. ii. 6.

235. Ah! these blessed considerations and scriptures, with many others of like nature, were in those days made to spangle in mine eyes; so that I have cause to say, **Praise ye the Lord. Praise God in His sanctuary, praise Him in the firmament of His power; praise Him for His mighty acts: praise Him according to His excellent greatness**. Psalm cl. 1, 2.

236. Having thus in a few words given you

a taste of the sorrow and affliction that my soul went under, by the guilt and terror that this my wicked thought did lay me under; and having given you also a touch of my deliverance therefrom, and of the sweet and blessed comfort that I met with afterwards, which comfort dwelt about a twelvemonth with my heart, to my unspeakable admiration: I will now (God willing), before I proceed any farther, give you in a word or two, what, as I conceive, was the cause of this temptation; and also after that, what advantage, at the last, it became unto my soul.

237. For the causes, I conceived they were principally two: of which two also I was deeply convinced all the time this trouble lay upon me. The first was, for that I did not, when I was delivered from the temptation that went before, still pray to God to to keep me from the temptations that were to come; for though, as I can say in truth, my soul was much in prayer before this trial seized me, yet then I prayed only, or at the

most principally, for the removal of present troubles, and for fresh discoveries of His love in Christ, which I saw afterwards was not enough to do; I also should have prayed that the great God would keep me from the evil that was to come.

238. Of this I was made deeply sensible by the prayer of holy **David**, who when he was under present mercy, yet prayed that God would hold him back from sin and temptation to come; **Then**, saith he, **shall I be upright**, **and I shall be innocent from the great transgression**. Psalm xix. 13. By this very word was I galled and condemned quite through this long temptation.

239. That was also another word that did much condemn me for my folly, in the neglect of this duty. Heb. iv. 16: **Let us therefore come boldly unto the throne of grace**, **that we may obtain mercy**, **and find grace to help in time of need**. This I had not done, and therefore was thus suffered to sin and fall, according to what is written, **Pray that**

ye enter not into temptation. And truly this very thing is to this day of such weight and awe upon me, that I dare not, when I come before the Lord, go of my knees, until I intreat Him for help and mercy against the temptations that are to come; and I do beseech thee, reader, that thou learn to beware of my negligence, by the afflictions, that for this thing I did for days, and months, and years, with sorrow undergo.

240. Another cause of this temptation was, that I had tempted God; and on this manner did I do it: Upon a time my wife was great with child, and before her full time was come, her pangs, as of a woman in travail, were fierce and strong upon her, even as if she would have fallen immediately in labour, and been delivered of an untimely birth: now at this very time it was, that I had been so strongly tempted to question the being of God; wherefore, as my wife lay crying by me, I said, but with all secrecy imaginable, even thinking in my heart,

Lord, if Thou wilt now remove this sad affliction from my wife, and cause that she be troubled no more therewith this night (and now were her pangs just upon her), **then I shall know that Thou canst discern the most secret thoughts of the heart**.

241. I had no sooner said it in my heart, but her pangs were taken from her, and she was cast into a deep sleep, and so continued till morning; at this I greatly marvelled, not knowing what to think; but after I had been awake a good while, and heard her cry no more, I fell asleep also; so when I awaked in the morning, it came upon me again, even what I had said in my heart the last night, and how the Lord had showed me, that He knew my secret thoughts, which was a great astonishment unto me for several weeks after.

242. Well, about a year and a half afterwards, that wicked sinful thought, of which I have spoken before, went through

my wicked heart, even this thought, **Let Christ go, if He will**: so when I was fallen under the guilt for this, the remembrance of my other thought, and of the effect thereof, would also come upon me with this retort, which also carried rebuke along with it, **Now you may see that God doth know the most secret thoughts of the heart**.

243. And with this, that of the passages that were betwixt the Lord, and His servant **Gideon**, fell upon my spirit; how because that **Gideon** tempted God with his fleece, both wet and dry, when he should have believed and ventured upon His word; therefore the Lord did afterwards so try him, as to send him against an innumerable company of enemies, and that too, as to outward appearance, without any strength or help. Judges vi. 7. Thus He served me, and that justly, for I should have believed His word, and not have put an **if** upon the all-seeingness of God.

244. And now to show you something

of the advantages that I also have gained by this temptation: and first, by this I was made continually to possess in my soul a very wonderful sense both of the blessing and glory of God, and of His beloved Son; in the temptation that went before, my soul was perplexed with unbelief, blasphemy, hardness of heart, questions about the being of God, Christ, the truth of the word, and certainty of the world to come: I say, then I was greatly assaulted and tormented with atheism, but now the case was otherwise; now was God and Christ continually before my face, though not in a way of comfort, but in a way of exceeding dread and terror. The glory of the holiness of God, did at this time break me to pieces; and the bowels and compassion of Christ did break me as on the wheel; for I could not consider Him but as a lost and rejected Christ, the remembrance of which, was as the continual breaking of my bones.

245. The scriptures also were wonderful

things unto me; I saw that the truth and verity of them were the keys of the kingdom of heaven; **those** that the scriptures favour, **they** must inherit bliss; but **those** that they oppose and condemn, **must** perish for evermore: Oh! this word, **For the scriptures cannot be broken**, would rend the caul of my heart: and so would that other, **Whose sins ye remit**, **they are remitted**; **but whose sins ye retain**, **they are retained**. Now I saw the apostles to be the elders of the city of refuge. Joshua xx. 4. Those that they were to receive in, were received to life; but those that they shut out, were to be slain by the avenger of blood.

246. Oh! one sentence of the scripture did more afflict and terrify my mind, I mean those sentences that stood against me (as sometimes I thought they every one did) more, I say, than an army of forty thousand men that might have come against me. Woe be to him against whom the scriptures bend themselves!

247. By this temptation I was made to see more into the nature of the promises than ever I was before; for I lying now trembling under the mighty hand of God, continually torn and rent by the thundering of His justice: this made me with careful heart, and watchful eye, with great fearfulness to turn over every leaf, and with much diligence, mixed with trembling, to consider every sentence, together with its natural force and latitude.

248. By this temptation also I was greatly holden off from my former foolish practice of putting by the word of promise when saw it came into my mind; for now, though I could not suck that comfort and sweetness from the promise, as I had done at other times; yet, like to a man sinking, I would catch at all I saw: formerly I thought I might not meddle with the promise, unless I felt its comfort, but now 'twas no time thus to do; the avenger of blood too hardly did pursue me.

249. Now therefore I was glad to catch at

that word which yet I feared I had no ground or right to own; and even to leap into the bosom of that promise that yet I feared did shut its heart against me. Now also I should labour to take the word as God hath laid it down, without restraining the natural force of one syllable thereof: O! what did I now see in that blessed sixth of John: **And him that cometh to me, I will in no wise cast out**. John vi. 37. Now I began to consider with myself, that God hath a bigger mouth to speak with, than I had a heart to conceive with; I thought also with myself, that He spake not His words in haste, or in an unadvised heat, but with infinite wisdom and judgment, and in very truth and faithfulness. 2 Sam. iii. 28.

250. I should in these days, often in my greatest agonies, even flounce towards the promise (as the horses do towards sound ground, that yet stick in the mire); concluding (though as one almost bereft of his wits through fear) on this I will rest and stay, and

leave the fulfilling of it to the God of heaven that made it. Oh! many a pull hath my heart had with Satan, for that blessed sixth of John: I did not now, as at other times, look principally for comfort (though, O how welcome would it have been unto me!). But now a word, a word to lean a weary soul upon, that it might not sink for ever! 'twas that I hunted for.

251. Yea, often when I have been making to the promise, I have seen as if the Lord would refuse my soul for ever; I was often as if I had run upon the pikes, and as if the Lord had thrust at me, to keep me from Him, as with a flaming sword. Then I should think of **Esther**, who went to petition the king contrary to the law. Esther iv. 16. I thought also of Benhadad's servants, who went with ropes upon their heads to their enemies for mercy. 1 Kings xx. 31, etc. The woman of Canaan also, that would not be daunted, though called dog by Christ, Matt. xv., 22, etc., and the man that went to borrow bread at midnight, Luke xi. 5–8, etc., were great

encouragements unto me.

252. I never saw those heights and depths in grace, and love, and mercy, as I saw after this temptation; great sins to draw out great grace; and where guilt is most terrible and fierce, there the mercy of God in Christ, when showed to the soul, appears most high and mighty. When **Job** had passed through his captivity, **he had twice as much as he had before**. Job xlii. 10. Blessed be God for Jesus Christ our Lord. Many other things I might here make observation of, but I would be brief, and therefore shall at this time omit them; and do pray God that my harms may make others fear to offend, lest they also be made to bear the iron yoke as I did.

I had two or three times, at or about my deliverance from this temptation, such strange apprehensions of the grace of God, that I could hardly bear up under it: it was so out of measure amazing, when I thought it could reach me, that I do think if that sense of it had abode long upon me, it would have made me incapable for business.

253. Now I shall go forward to give you a relation of other of the Lord's dealings with me at sundry other seasons, and of the temptations I then did meet withal. I shall begin with what I met with when first I did join in fellowship with the people of God in **Bedford**. After I had propounded to the church, that my desire was to walk in the order and ordinances of Christ with them, and was also admitted by them: while I thought of that blessed ordinance of Christ, which was His last supper with His disciples before His death, that scripture, **Do this in remembrance of Me**, Luke xxii. 19, was made a very precious word unto me; for by it the Lord did come down upon my conscience with the discovery of His death for my sins; and as I then felt, did as if He plunged me in the virtue of the same. But behold, I had not been long a partaker at that ordinance, but such fierce and sad temptations did attend me at all times therein, both to blaspheme the

ordinance, and to wish some deadly thing to those that then did eat thereof: that lest I should at any time be guilty of consenting to these wicked and fearful thoughts, I was forced to bend myself all the while, to pray to God to keep me from such blasphemies: and also to cry to God to bless the bread and cup to them, as it went from mouth to mouth. The reason of this temptation, I have thought since, was, because I did not with that reverence that became me at first, approach to partake thereof.

254. Thus I continued for three quarters of a year, and could never have rest nor ease: but at the last the Lord came in upon my soul with that same scripture, by which my soul was visited before: and after that, I have been usually very well and comfortable in the partaking of that blessed ordinance; and have, I trust, therein discerned the Lord's body, as broken for my sins, and that His precious blood hath been shed for my transgressions.

255. Upon a time I was something inclining to a consumption, wherewith about the spring I was suddenly and violently seized, with much weakness in my outward man; insomuch that I thought I could not live. Now began I afresh to give myself up to a serious examination after my state and condition for the future, and of my evidences for that blessed world to come: for it hath, I bless the name of God, been my usual course, as always, so especially in the day of affliction, to endeavour to keep my interest in the life to come, clear before mine eyes.

256. But I had no sooner began to recall to mind my former experience of the goodness of God to my soul, but there came flocking into my mind an innumerable company of my sins and transgressions; amongst which these were at this time most to my affliction; namely, my deadness, dulness, and coldness in holy duties; my wanderings of heart, of my wearisomeness in all good things, my want of love to God, His ways and people, with

this at the end of all, **Are these the fruits of Christianity? Are these tokens of a blessed man**?

257. At the apprehensions of these things my sickness was doubled upon me; for now I was sick in my inward man, my soul was clogged with guilt; now also was my former experience of God's goodness to me, quite taken out of my mind, and hid as if they had never been, or seen: now was my soul greatly pinched between these two considerations, **Live I must not**, **die I dare not**. Now I sunk and fell in my spirit, and was giving up all for lost; but as I was walking up and down in the house as a man in a most woeful state, that word of God took hold of my heart, **Ye are justified freely by His grace, through the redemption that is in Christ Jesus**. Rom. iii. 24. But oh! what a turn it made upon me!

258. Now was I as one awaked out of some troublesome sleep and dream; and listening to this heavenly sentence, I was as if I had heard it thus expounded to me:

Sinner, thou thinkest, that because thy sins and infirmities, I cannot save thy soul; but behold My Son is by me, and upon Him I look, and not on thee, and shall deal with thee according as I am pleased with Him. At this I was greatly lightened in my mind, and made to understand, that God could justify a sinner at any time; it was but His looking upon Christ, and imputing His benefits to us, and the work was forthwith done.

259. And as I was thus in a muse, that scripture also came with great power upon my spirit, **Not by works of righteousness that we have done, but according to His mercy He hath saved us, etc.** 2 Tim. i. 9; Tit. iii. 5. Now was I got on high, I saw myself within the arms of grace and mercy; and though I was before afraid to think of a dying hour, yet, now I cried, **Let me die**: Now death was lovely and beautiful in my sight, for I saw **We shall never live indeed, till we be gone to the other world.** Oh! methought

this life is but a slumber, in comparison with that above. At this time also I saw more in these words, **Heirs of God**, Rom. viii. 17, than ever I shall be able to express while I live in this world: **Heirs of God**! God Himself is the portion of the saints. This I saw and wondered at, but cannot tell you what I saw.

260. Again, as I was at another time very ill and weak, all that time also the tempter did beset me strongly (for I find he is much for assaulting the soul; when it begins to approach towards the grave, then is his opportunity), labouring to hide from me my former experience of God's goodness: also setting before me the terrors of death, and the judgment of God, insomuch that at this time, through my fear of miscarrying for ever (should I now die), I was as one dead before death came, and was as if I had felt myself already descending into the pit; methought I said, There were no way, but to hell I must: but behold, just as I was in the midst of those fears, these

words of the angel's carrying **Lazarus** into **Abraham's** bosom darted in upon me, as who should say, **So it shall be with thee when thou dost leave this world**. This did sweetly revive my spirit, and help me to hope in God; which when I had with comfort mused on a while, that word fell with great weight upon my mind, **O death, where is thy sting**? **O grave, where is thy victory**? 1 Cor. xv. 55. At this I became both well in body and mind at once, for my sickness did presently vanish, and I walked comfortably in my work for God again.

261. At another time, though just before I was pretty well and savoury in my spirit, yet suddenly there fell upon me a great cloud of darkness, which did so hide from me the things of God and Christ, that I was as if I had never seen or known them in my life: I was also so over-run in my soul with a senseless heartless frame of spirit, that I could not feel my soul to move or stir after **grace** and **life** by **Christ**; I was as if my loins were broken,

or as if my hands and feet had been tied or bound with chains. At this time also I felt some weakness to seize upon my outward man, which made still the other affliction the more heavy and uncomfortable to me.

262. After I had been in this condition some three or four days, as I was sitting by the fire, I suddenly felt this word to sound in my heart, **I must go to Jesus**. At this my former darkness and atheism fled away, and the blessed things of heaven were set in my view. While I was on this sudden thus overtaken with surprise, Wife (said I), is there ever such a scripture, **I must go to Jesus**? She said, she could not tell; therefore I sat musing still, to see if I could remember such a place: I had not sat above two or three minutes, but that came bolting in upon me, **And to an innumerable company of angels**; and withal, Hebrews twelfth, about the mount **Sion**, was set before mine eyes. Heb. xii. 22–24.

263. Then with joy I told my wife, **O! now**

I know, **I know**! But that night was a good night to me, I never had but few better; I longed for the company of some of God's people, that I might have imparted unto them what God had showed me. Christ was a precious Christ to my soul that night; I could scarce lie in my bed for joy, and peace, and triumph, through Christ. This great glory did not continue upon me until morning, yet the twelfth of the Author to the Hebrews, Heb. xii. 22, 23, was a blessed scripture to me for many days together after this.

264. The words are these: **Ye are come to mount Sion**, **and unto the city of the living God**, **the heavenly Jerusalem**, **and to an innumerable company of angels**, **to the general assembly and church of the first-born**, **which are written in heaven; and to God the Judge of all**, **and to the spirits of just men made perfect**, **and to Jesus the Mediator of the New Covenant**, **and to the blood of sprinkling**, **that speaketh better things than that of Abel**. Through this

blessed sentence the Lord led me over and over, first to this word, and then to that; and showed me wonderful glory in every one of them. These words also have oft since that time, been great refreshment to my spirit. Blessed be God for having mercy on me.

A Brief Account of the Author's Call to the Work of the Ministry

265. AND NOW I AM SPEAKING my experience, I will in this place thrust in a word or two concerning my preaching the word, and of God's dealing with me in that particular also. For after I had been about five or six years awakened, and helped myself to see both the want and worth of Jesus Christ our Lord, and also enabled to venture my soul upon Him; some of the

most able among the saints with us, I say, the most able for judgment and holiness of life, as they conceived, did perceive that God had counted me worth to understand something of His will in His holy and blessed word, and had given me utterance in some measure, to express what I saw to others, for edification; therefore they desired me, and that with much earnestness, that I would be willing, at sometimes to take in hand, in one of the meetings, to speak a word of exhortation unto them.

266. The which, though at the first it did much dash and abash my spirit, yet being still by them desired and entreated, I consented to their request, and did twice at two several assemblies (but in private), though with much weakness and infirmity, discover my gift amongst them; at which they not only seemed to be, but did solemnly protest, as in the sight of the great God, they were both affected and comforted; and gave thanks to the Father of mercies, for the grace bestowed

on me.

267. After this, sometimes, when some of them did go into the country to teach, they would also that I should go with them; where, though as yet, I did not nor durst not, make use of my gift in an open way, yet more privately, still, as I came amongst the good people in those places, I did sometimes speak a word of admonition unto them also; the which they, as the other, received with rejoicing at the mercy of God to me-ward, professing their souls were edified thereby.

268. Wherefore, to be brief; at last, being still desired by the church, after some solemn prayer to the Lord, with fasting, I was more particularly called forth, and appointed to a more ordinary and public preaching of the word, not only to and amongst them that believed, but also to offer the gospel to those who had not yet received the faith thereof; about which time I did evidently find in my mind a secret pricking forward thereto; though I bless God, not for desire

of vain-glory; for at that time I was most sorely afflicted with the fiery darts of the devil, concerning my eternal state.

269. But yet could not be content, unless I was found in the exercise of my gift, unto which also I was greatly animated, not only by the continual desires of the godly, but also by that saying of **Paul** to the **Corinthians**: **I beseech you, brethren (ye know the household of Stephanas, that it is the first fruits of Achaia, and that they have addicted themselves to the ministry of the saints) that ye submit yourselves unto such, and to every one that helpeth with us, and laboureth**. 1 Cor. xvi. 15, 16.

270. By this text I was made to see that the Holy Ghost never intended that men who have gifts and abilities, should bury them in the earth, but rather did command and stir up such to the exercise of their gift, and also did commend those that were apt and ready so to do. **They have addicted themselves to the ministry of the saints**. This scripture, in

these days, did continually run in my mind, to encourage me, and strengthen me in this my work for God; I have also been encouraged from several other scriptures and examples of the godly, both specified in the word, and other ancient histories: **Acts** viii. 4 and xviii. 24, 25, etc.; 1 **Pet.** iv. 10; **Rom.** xii. 6; **Fox's Acts** and **Mon.**

271. Wherefore, though of myself of all the saints the most unworthy; yet I, but with great fear and trembling at the sight of my own weakness, did set upon the work, and did according to my gift, and the proportion of my faith, preach that blessed gospel that God had showed me in the holy word of truth: which when the country understood, they came in to hear the word by hundreds, and that from all parts, though upon sundry and divers accounts.

272. And I thank God, He gave unto me some measure of bowels and pity for their souls, which also did put me forward to labour, with great diligence and

earnestness, to find out such a word as might, if God would bless, lay hold of, and awaken the conscience; in which also the good Lord had respect to the desire of His servant; for I had not preached long, before some began to be touched, and be greatly afflicted in their minds at the apprehension of the greatness of their sin, and of their need of Jesus Christ.

273. But I first could not believe that God should speak by me to the heart of any man, still counting myself unworthy; yet those who thus were touched, would love me and have a particular respect for me; and though I did put it from me, that they should be awakened by me, still they would confess it, and affirm it before the saints of God: they would also bless God for me (unworthy wretch that I am!) and count me God's instrument that showed to them the way of salvation.

274. Wherefore seeing them in both their words and deeds to be so constant, and also in their hearts so earnestly pressing

after the knowledge of Jesus Christ, rejoicing that ever God did send me where they were; then I began to conclude it might be so, that God had owned in His work such a foolish one as I; and then came that word of God to my heart, with much sweet refreshment, **The blessing of him that was ready to perish, is come upon me; and I caused the widow's heart to sing for joy**. Job xxix. 13.

275. At this therefore I rejoiced; yea, the tears of those whom God did awaken by my preaching, would be both solace and encouragement to me: for I thought on those sayings, **Who is He then that maketh me glad, but the same which is made sorry by Me**? 2 Cor. ii. 2. And again, **If I be not an Apostle to others, yet doubtless, I am unto you: for the seal of mine apostleship are ye in the Lord**. 1 Cor. ix. 2. These things, therefore, were as another argument unto me, that God had called me to, and stood by me in this work.

276. In my preaching of the word, I took special notice of this one thing, namely, that the Lord did lead me to begin where His word begins with sinners; that is, to condemn all flesh, and to open and allege, that the curse of God by the law, doth belong to, and lay hold on all men as they come into the world, because of sin. Now this part of my work I fulfilled with great sense; for the terrors of the law, and guilt for my transgressions, lay heavy on my conscience: I preached what I felt, what I smartingly did feel; even that under which my poor soul did groan and tremble to astonishment.

277. Indeed, I have been as one sent to them from the dead; I went myself in chains, to preach to them in chains; and carried that fire in my own conscience, that I persuaded them to be aware of. I can truly say, and that without dissembling, that when I have been to preach, I have gone full of guilt and terror, even to the pulpit door, and there it hath been taken off, and I have been at liberty in

my mind until I have done my work; and then immediately, even before I could get down the pulpit stairs, I have been as bad as I was before; yet God carried me on, but surely with a strong hand, for neither guilt nor hell could take me off my work.

278. Thus I went on for the space of two years, crying out against men's sins, and their fearful state because of them. After which, the Lord came in upon my own soul, with some staid peace and comfort through Christ; for He did give me many sweet discoveries of His blessed grace through Him; wherefore now I altered in my preaching (for still I preached what I saw and felt); now therefore I did much labour to hold forth Jesus Christ in all His offices, relations, and benefits unto the world; and did strive also to discover, to condemn, and remove those false supports and props on which the world doth both lean, and by them fall and perish. On these things also I staid as long as on the other.

279. After this, God led me into something of

the mystery of the union of Christ; wherefore that I discovered and showed to them also. And, when I had travelled through these three chief points of the word of God, about the space of five years or more, I was caught in my present practice, and cast into prison, where I have lain above as long again to confirm the truth by way of suffering, as I was before in testifying of it according to the scriptures, in a way of preaching.

280. When I have been in preaching, I thank God my heart hath often all the time of this and the other exercise, with great earnestness cried to God that He would make the word effectual to the salvation of the soul; still being grieved lest the enemy should take the word away from the conscience, and so it should become unfruitful: wherefore I should labour to speak the word, as that thereby, if it were possible, the sin and person guilty might be particularized by it.

281. And when I have done the exercise, it hath gone to my heart, to think the word

should now fall as rain on stony places; still wishing from my heart, Oh! that they who have heard me speak this day, did but see as I do, what sin, death, hell, and the curse of God is; and also what the grace, and love, and mercy of God is, through Christ, to men in such a case as they are, who are yet estranged from Him. And indeed, I did often say in my heart before the Lord, **That if to be hanged up presently before their eyes**, **would be a means to awaken them**, **and confirm them in the truth**, **I gladly should be contented**.

282. For I have been in my preaching, especially when I have been engaged in the doctrine of life by Christ, without works, as if an angel of God had stood by at my back to encourage me: Oh! it hath been with such power and heavenly evidence upon my own soul, while I have been labouring to unfold it, to demonstrate it, and to fasten it upon the conscience of others; that I could not be contented with saying, **I believe**, **and**

---

am sure; methought I was more than sure (if it be lawful to express myself) that those things which then I asserted, were true.

283. When I first went to preach the word abroad, the doctors and priests of the country did open wide against me. But I was persuaded of this, not to render railing for railing; but to see how many of their carnal professors I could convince of their miserable state by the law, and of the want and worth of Christ: for, thought I, **This shall answer for me in time to come**, **when they shall be for my hire before their face**. Gen. xxx. 33.

284. I never cared to meddle with things that were controverted, and in dispute among the saints, especially things of the lowest nature; yet it pleased me much to contend with great earnestness for the word of faith, and the remission of sins by the death and sufferings of Jesus: but I say, as to other things, I should let them alone, because I saw they engendered strife; and because that

they neither in doing, nor in leaving undone, did commend us to God to be His: besides, I saw my work before me did run into another channel, even to carry an awakening word; to that therefore did I stick and adhere.

285. I never endeavoured to, nor durst make use of other men's lines, Rom. xv. 18 (though I condemn not all that do), for I verily thought, and found by experience, that what was taught me by the word and Spirit of Christ, could be spoken, maintained, and stood to, by the soundest and best established conscience; and though I will not now speak all that I know in this matter, yet my experience hath more interest in that text of scripture, Gal. i. 11, 12, than many amongst men are aware.

286. If any of those who were awakened by my ministry, did after that fall back (as sometimes too many did), I can truly say, their loss hath been more to me, than if one of my own children, begotten of my own body, had been going to its grave: I think

verily, I may speak it without any offence to the Lord, nothing has gone so near me as that; unless it was the fear of the loss of the salvation of my own soul. I have counted as if I had goodly buildings and lordships in those places where my children were born; my heart hath been so wrapped up in the glory of this excellent work, that I counted myself more blessed and honoured of God by this, than if He had made me the emperor of the Christian world, or the lord of all the glory of the earth without it! Oh these words! **He which converteth the sinner from the error of his way, shall save a soul from death.** James v. 20. **The fruit of the righteous is a tree of life; and he that winneth souls is wise.** Prov. xi. 30. **They that be wise shall shine as the brightness of the firmament, and they that turn many to righteousness, as the stars for ever and ever.** Dan. xii. 3. **For what is our hope, or joy, or crown of rejoicing? Are not even ye in the presence of our Lord**

Jesus Christ at His coming? **For ye are our glory and joy**. 1 Thes. ii. 19, 20. These, I say, with many others of a like nature, have been great refreshments to me.

287. I have observed, that where I have had a work to do for God, I have had first, as it were, the going of God upon my spirit, to desire I might preach there: I have also observed, that such and such souls in particular, have been strongly set upon my heart, and I stirred up to wish for their salvation; and that these very souls have, after this, been given in as the fruits of my ministry. I have observed, that a word cast in, by-the-bye, hath done more execution in a sermon, than all that was spoken besides: sometimes also, when I have thought I did no good, then I did the most of all; and at other times, when I thought I should catch them, I have fished for nothing.

288. I have also observed, that where there has been a work to do upon sinners, there the devil hath begun to roar in the

hearts and by the mouths of his servants: yea, oftentimes, when the wicked world hath raged most, there hath been souls awakened by the word: I could instance particulars, but I forbear.

289. My great desire in my fulfilling my ministry was to get into the darkest places of the country, even amongst those people that were farthest off of profession; yet not because I could not endure the light (for I feared not to show my gospel to any) but because I found my spirit did lean most after awakening and converting work, and the word that I carried did lean itself most that way also; **Yea, so have I strived to preach the gospel, not where Christ was named, lest I should build upon another man's foundation**. Rom. xv. 20.

290. In my preaching I have really been in pain, and have, as it were, travailed to bring forth children to God; neither could I be satisfied unless some fruits did appear in my work. If I were fruitless, it mattered not

who commanded me: but if I were fruitful, I cared not who did condemn. I have thought of that: **Lo! children are an heritage of the Lord**; **and the fruit of the womb is His reward**. – **As arrows are in the hand of a mighty man**, **so are children of the youth**. **Happy is the man that hath his quiver full of them**: **they shall not be ashamed**, **but they shall speak with the enemies in the gate**. Psalm cxxvii. 3–5.

291. It pleased me nothing to see people drink in opinions, if they seemed ignorant of Jesus Christ, and the worth of their own salvation, sound conviction for sin, especially for unbelief, and a heart set on fire to be saved by Christ, with strong breathings after a truly sanctified soul: that it was that delighted me; those were the souls I counted blessed.

292. But in this work, as in all other, I had my temptations attending me, and that of divers kinds; as sometimes I should be assaulted with great discouragement therein, fearing that I should not be able to speak a word

at all to edification; nay, that I should not be able to speak sense unto the people; at which times I should have such a strange faintness and strengthlessness seize upon my body, that my legs have scarce been able to carry me to the place of exercise.

293. Sometimes again when I have been preaching, I have been violently assaulted with thoughts of blasphemy, and strongly tempted to speak the words with my mouth before the congregation. I have also at some times, even when I have begun to speak the word with much clearness, evidence, and liberty of speech, yet been, before the ending of that opportunity, so blinded and so estranged from the things I have been speaking, and have been also so straightened in my speech, as to utterance before the people, that I have been as if I had not known, or remembered what I have been about; or as if my head had been in a bag all the time of my exercise.

294. Again, when as sometimes I have

been about to preach upon some smart and searching portion of the word, I have found the tempter suggest, **What! will you preach this! This condemns yourself**; **of this your own soul is guilty**; **wherefore preach not of it at all**; **or if you do**, **yet so mince it**, **as to make way for your own escape**; **lest instead of awakening others**, **you lay that guilt upon your own soul**, **that you will never get from under**.

295. But I thank the Lord, I have been kept from consenting to these so horrid suggestions, and have rather, as Sampson, bowed myself with all my might, to condemn sin and transgression, wherever I found it; yea, though therein also I did bring guilt upon my own conscience: **Let me die** (thought I), **with the Philistines**, Judges xvi. 29, 30, rather than deal corruptly with the blessed word of God. **Thou that teachest another**, **teachest thou not thyself**? It is far better that thou do judge thyself, even by preaching plainly unto others, than that

thou, to save thyself, imprison the truth in righteousness. Blessed be God for His help also in this.

296. I have also, while found in this blessed work of Christ, been often tempted to pride and liftings up of heart: and though I dare not say, I have not been affected with this, yet truly the Lord of His precious mercy, hath so carried it towards me, that for the most part I have had but small joy to give way to such a thing: for it hath been my every day's portion to be let into the evil of my own heart, and still made to see such a multitude of corruptions and infirmities therein, that it hath caused hanging down of the head under all my gifts and attainments; I have felt this thorn in the flesh, 2 Cor. xii. 8, 9, the very mercy of God to me.

297. I have also had, together with this, some notable place or other of the word presented before me, which word hath contained in it some sharp and piercing sentence concerning the perishing of the

soul, notwithstanding gifts and parts: as, for instance, that hath been of great use to me: **Though I speak with the tongues of men and angels**, **and have not charity**, **I am become as sounding brass**, **and a tinkling cymbal**. 1 Cor. xiii. 1, 2.

298. A tinkling cymbal is an instrument of music, with which a skilful player can make such melodious and heart-inflaming music, that all who hear him play, can scarcely hold from dancing; and yet behold the cymbal hath not life, neither comes the music from it, but because of the art of him that plays therewith; so then the instrument at last may come to nought and perish, though in times past such music hath been made upon it.

299. Just thus I saw it was, and will be, with them who have gifts, but want saving grace; they are in the hand of Christ, as the cymbal in the hand of **David**: and as **David** could with the cymbal make that mirth in the service of God, as to elevate the hearts of the worshippers, so Christ can use these

gifted men, as with them to affect the souls of His people in His church; yet when He hath done all, hang them by, as lifeless, though sounding cymbals.

300. This consideration therefore, together with some others, were for the most part, as a maul on the head of pride, and desire of vain-glory. What, thought I, shall I be proud because I am a sounding brass? Is it so much to be a fiddle? hath not the least creature that hath life, more of God in it than these? Besides, I knew 'twas love should never die, but these must cease and vanish: so I concluded, a little grace, a little love, a little of the true fear of God, is better than all the gifts: yea, and I am fully convinced of it, that it is possible for souls that can scarce give a man an answer, but with great confusion as to method; I say, it is possible for them to have a thousand times more grace, and so to be more in the love and favour of the Lord, than some who by the virtue of the gift of knowledge, can deliver themselves like

angels.

301. Thus therefore I came to perceive that, though gifts in themselves were good, to the thing for which they are designed, to wit, the edification of others; yet empty, and without power to save the soul of him that hath them, if they be **alone**: neither are they, as so, any sign of a man's state to be happy, being only a dispensation of God to some, of whose improvement, or non-improvement, they must when a little love more is over, give an account to Him that is ready to judge the quick and the dead.

302. This showed me too, that gifts being alone, were dangerous, not in themselves, but because of those evils that attend them that have them, to wit, pride, desire of vain glory, self-conceit, etc., all which were easily blown up at the applause and commendation of every unadvised Christian, to the endangering of a poor creature to fall into the condemnation of the devil.

303. I saw therefore that he that hath gifts,

had need be let into a sight of the nature of them, to wit, that they come short of making of him to be in a truly saved condition, lest he rest in them, and so fall short of the grace of God.

304. He hath cause also to walk humbly with God and be little in his own eyes, and to remember withal, that his gifts are not his own, but the churches; and that by them he is made a servant to the church; and he must also give at last an account of his stewardship unto the Lord Jesus, and to give a good account will be a blessed thing.

305. Let all men therefore prize a little with the fear of the Lord (gifts indeed are desirable), but yet great grace and small gifts are better than great gifts and no grace. It doth not say, the Lord gives gifts and glory, but the Lord gives grace and glory; and blessed is such an one, to whom the Lord gives grace, true grace; for that is a certain forerunner of glory.

306. But when Satan perceived that his

thus tempting and assaulting of me, would not answer his design; to wit, to overthrow the ministry, and make it ineffectual, as to the ends thereof: then he tried another way, which was, to stir up the minds of the ignorant and malicious to load me with slanders and reproaches: now therefore I may say, that what the devil could devise, and his instruments invent, was whirled up and down the country against me, thinking, as I said, that by that means they should make my ministry to be abandoned.

307. It began therefore to be rumoured up and down among the people, that I was a witch, a Jesuit, a highwayman, and the like.

308. To all which, I shall only say, God knows that I am innocent. But as for mine accusers, let them provide themselves to meet me before the tribunal of the Son of God, there to answer for all these things (with all the rest of their iniquities) unless God shall give them repentance for them, for the which I pray with all my heart.

309. But that which was reported with the boldest confidence, was, that I had my **misses**, my **whores**, my **bastards**; yea, **two wives** at once, and the like. Now these slanders (with the others) I glory in, because but slanders, foolish or knavish lies, and falsehoods cast upon me by the devil and his seed; and, should I not be dealt with thus wickedly by the world, I should want one sign of a saint, and a child of God. **Blessed are ye** (said the Lord Jesus) **when men shall revile you and persecute you, and shall say all manner of evil against you falsely for My sake; rejoice and be exceeding glad, for great is your reward in heaven, for so persecuted they the prophets which were before you**. Matt. iv. 11.

310. These things therefore, upon mine own account, trouble me not; no, though they were twenty times more than they are. I have a good conscience, and whereas they speak evil of me, as an evil-doer, they shall be ashamed that falsely accuse my

good conversation in Christ.

311. So then, what shall I say to those who have thus bespattered me? Shall I threaten them? Shall I chide them? Shall I flatter them? Shall I entreat them to hold their tongues? No, not I. Were it not for that these things make them ripe for damnation, that are the authors and abettors, I would say unto them, **Report it**, because 'twill increase my glory.

312. Therefore I bind these lies and slanders to me as an ornament; it belongs to my Christian profession to be vilified, slandered, reproached and reviled; and since all this is nothing else, as my God and my conscience do bear me witness, I rejoice in reproaches for Christ's sake.

313. I also call all these fools or knaves, that have thus made it any thing of their business to affirm any of the things afore-named of me; namely, That I have been naught with other women, or the like. When they have used the utmost of their

endeavours, and made the fullest inquiry that they can, to prove against me truly, that there is any woman in heaven, or earth, or hell, that can say, I have at any time, in any place, by day or night, so much as attempted to be naught with them; and speak I thus to beg my enemies into a good esteem of me? No, not I: I will in this beg belief of no man: believe or disbelieve me in this, all is a-case to me.

314. My foes have missed their mark in this shooting at me: I am not the man: I wish that they themselves be guiltless. If all the fornicators and adulterers in **England** were hanged up by the neck till they be dead, **John Bunyan**, the object of their envy, would be still alive and well. I know not whether there be such a thing as a woman breathing under the copes of the whole heaven, but by their apparel, their children, or by common fame, except my wife.

315. And in this I admire the wisdom of God, that He made me shy of women from

my first conversion until now. Those shy of women know, and can also bear me witness, with whom I have been most intimately concerned, that it is a rare thing to see me carry it pleasant towards a woman: the common salutation of women I abhor; 'tis odious to me in whomsoever I see it. Their company alone, I cannot away with; I seldom so much as touch a woman's hand; for I think these things are not so becoming me. When I have seen good men salute those women that they have visited, or that have visited them, I have at times made my objection against it; and when they have answered, that it was but a piece of civility, I have told them, it is not a comely sight. Some indeed have urged the holy kiss; but then I have asked why they made baulks? why they did salute the most handsome, and let the ill-favoured go? Thus, how laudable soever such things have been in the eyes of others, they have been unseemly in my sight.

316. And now for a wind-up in this matter,

I calling not only men, but angels, to prove me guilty of having carnally to do with any woman save my wife: nor am I afraid to do it a second time; knowing that it cannot offend the Lord in such a case, to call God for a record upon my soul, that in these things I am innocent. Not that I have been thus kept, because of any goodness in me, more than any other; but God has been merciful to me, and has kept me; to whom I pray that He will keep me still, not only from this, but every evil way and work, and preserve me to His heavenly kingdom. **Amen**.

317. Now as Satan laboured by reproaches and slanders, to make me vile among my countrymen; that, if possible, my preaching might be made of none effect; so there was added hereto, a long and tedious imprisonment, that thereby I might be frightened from my service for Christ, and the world terrified, and made afraid to hear me preach; of which I shall in the next place give you a brief account.

A Brief Account of the Author's Imprisonment

318. HAVING MADE PROFESSION of the glorious gospel of Christ a long time, and preached the same about five years, I was apprehended at a meeting of good people in the country (among whom, had they let me alone, I should have preached that day, but they took me away from amongst them), and had me before a justice; who, after I had offered security for my appearing at the

next sessions, yet committed me, because my sureties would not consent to be bound that I should preach no more to the people.

319. At the sessions after I was indicted for an upholder and maintainer of unlawful assemblies and conventicles, and for not conforming to the national worship of the church of **England**; and after some conference there with the justices, they taking my plain dealing with them for a confession, as they termed it, **of the indictment, did sentence me to a perpetual banishment, because I refused to conform**. So being again delivered up to the jailer's hands, I was had home to prison, and there have lain now complete twelve years, waiting to see what God would suffer these men to do with me.

320. In which condition I have continued with much content, through grace, but have met with many turnings and goings upon my heart, both from the Lord, Satan, and my own corruptions; by all which (glory be to Jesus

Christ) I have also received among many things, much conviction, instruction, and understanding, of which at large I shall not here discourse; only give you a hint or two, a word that may stir up the godly to bless God, and to pray for me; and also to take encouragement, should the case be their own – **not to fear what man can do unto them**.

321. I never had in all my life so great an inlet into the word of God as now: those scriptures that I saw nothing in before, are made in this place and state to shine upon me; Jesus Christ also was never more real and apparent than now; here I have seen and felt Him indeed: Oh! that word, **We have not preached unto you cunningly devised fables**, 2 Pet. i. 16, and that, **God raised Christ from the dead, and gave Him glory, that our faith and hope might be in God** 1 Pet. i. 21, were blessed words unto me in this my imprisoned condition.

322. These three or four scriptures also have

been great refreshments in this condition to me: John xiv. 1–4; John xvi. 33; Col. iii. 3, 4; Heb. xii. 22–24. So that sometimes when I have been in the savour of them, I have been able to laugh at destruction, **and to fear neither the horse nor his rider**. I have had sweet sights of the forgiveness of my sins in this place, and of my being with Jesus in another world: **Oh! the mount Sion, the heavenly Jerusalem, the innumerable company of angels, and God the Judge of all, and the spirits of just men made perfect, and Jesus,** have been sweet unto me in this place: I have seen that here, that I am persuaded I shall never, while in this world, be able to express: I have seen a truth in this scripture, **Whom having not seen, ye love; in whom, though now you see Him not, yet believing, ye rejoice with joy unspeakable, and full of glory**. 1 Pet. i. 8.

323. I never knew what it was for God to stand by me at all turns, and at every

offer of Satan to afflict me, etc., as I have found Him since I came in hither: for look how fears have presented themselves, so have supports and encouragements; yea, when I have started, even as it were, at nothing else but my shadow, yet God, as being very tender of me, hath not suffered me to be molested, but would with one scripture or another, strengthen me against all; insomuch that I have often said, **were it lawful, I could pray for greater trouble, for the greater comfort's sake**. Eccl. vii. 14; 2 Cor. i. 5.

324. Before I came to prison, I saw what was coming, and had especially two considerations warm upon my heart; the first was, how to be able to encounter death, should that be here my portion. For the first of these, that scripture, Col. i. 11, was great information to me, namely, to pray to God **to be strengthened with all might, according to His glorious power, unto all patience and long-suffering**

with joyfulness. I could seldom go to prayer before I was imprisoned; but for not so little as a year together, this sentence, or sweet petition would, as it were, thrust itself into my mind, and persuade me, that if ever I would go through long-suffering, I must have all patience, especially if I would endure it joyfully.

325. As to the second consideration, that saying (2 Cor. i. 9) was of great use to me, **But we had the sentence of death in ourselves, that we should not trust in ourselves, but in God, which raiseth the dead**. By this scripture I was made to see, That if ever I would suffer rightly, I must first pass a sentence of death upon every thing that can properly be called a thing of this life, even to reckon myself, my wife, my children, my health, my enjoyments, and all as dead to me, and myself as dead to them.

326. The second was to live upon God that is invisible, as Paul said in another place;

the way not to faint is, **To look not on the things that are seen, but at the things that are not seen; for the things that are seen are temporal, but the things that are not seen are eternal**. And thus I reasoned with myself, if I provide only for a prison, then the whip comes at unawares; and so doth also the pillory: Again, if I only provide for these, then I am not fit for banishment. Further, if I conclude that banishment is the worst, then if death comes, I am surprised: so that I see, the best way to go through sufferings, is to trust in God through Christ, as touching the world to come; and as touching this world, **to count the grave my house, to make my bed in darkness; to say to corruption, Thou art my father, and to the worm, Thou art my mother and sister**: that is, to familiarize these things to me.

327. But notwithstanding these helps, I found myself a man and compassed with infirmities; the parting with my wife and poor children, hath often been to me in

this place, as the pulling the flesh from the bones, and that not only because I am somewhat too fond of these great mercies, but also because I should have often brought to my mind the many hardships, miseries, and wants that my poor family was like to meet with, should I be taken from them, especially my poor blind child, who lay nearer my heart than all besides: Oh! the thoughts of the hardship I thought my poor blind one might go under, would break my heart to pieces.

328. Poor child! thought I, what sorrow art thou like to have for thy portion in this world! Thou must be beaten, must beg, suffer hunger, cold, nakedness, and a thousand calamities, though I cannot now endure the wind should blow upon thee. But yet recalling myself, thought I, I must venture you all with God, though it goeth to the quick to leave you: Oh! I saw in this condition I was as a man who was pulling down his house upon the head of his wife and children; yet, thought

I, I must do it, I must do it: and now I thought on those **two milch kine that were to carry the ark of God into another country, and to leave their calves behind them**. 1 Sam. vi. 10–12.

329. But that which helped me in this temptation, was divers considerations, of which, three in special here I will name, the first was the consideration of these two scriptures, **Leave thy fatherless children, I will preserve them alive, and let thy widows trust in me**: and again, **The Lord said, Verily it shall be well with thy remnant, verily, I will cause the enemy to entreat thee well in the time of evil, and in time of affliction**. Jer. xlix. 11; xv. 11.

330. I had also this consideration, that if I should not venture all for God, I engaged God to take care of my concernments: but if I forsook Him and His ways, for fear of any trouble that should come to me or mine, then I should not only falsify my profession, but should count also that my concernments

were not so sure, if left at God's feet, whilst I stood to and for His name, as they would be if they were under my own care, though with the denial of the way of God. This was a smarting consideration, and as spurs unto my flesh. That scripture also greatly helped it to fasten the more upon me, where Christ prays against Judas, that God would disappoint him in his selfish thoughts, which moved him to sell his Master. Pray read it soberly: Psalm cix. 6–8, etc.

331. I had also another consideration, and that was, the dread of the torments of hell, which I was sure they must partake of that for fear of the cross, do shrink from their profession of Christ, His words and laws before the sons of men: I thought also of the glory that He had prepared for those that in faith, and love, and patience, stood to His ways before them. These things, I say, have helped me, when the thoughts of the misery that both myself and mine, might for the sake of my profession be exposed to, hath

lain pinching on my mind.

332. When I have indeed conceited that I might be banished for my profession, then I have thought of that scripture: **They were stoned, they were sawn asunder, were tempted, were slain with the sword, they wandered about in sheep-skins, and goat-skins, being destitute, afflicted, tormented, of whom the world was not worthy**; for all they thought they were too bad to dwell and abide amongst them. I have also thought of that saying, **the Holy Ghost witnesseth in every city, that bonds and afflictions abide me**. I have verily thought that **my** soul and **it** have sometimes reasoned about the sore and sad estate of a banished and exiled condition, how they were exposed to hunger, to cold, to perils, to nakedness, to enemies, and a thousand calamities; and at last, it may be, to die in a ditch, like a poor and desolate sheep. But I thank God, hitherto I have not been moved by these most **delicate** reasonings, but have

rather, by them, more approved my heart to God.

333. I will tell you a pretty business: – I was once above all the rest, in a very sad and low condition for many weeks; at which time also, I being but a young prisoner, and not acquainted with the laws, had this lying much upon my spirits, **that my imprisonment might end at the gallows for ought that I could tell**. Now therefore Satan laid hard at me, to beat me out of heart, by suggesting thus unto me: **But how if**, **when you come indeed to die**, **you should be in this condition**; **that is**, **as not to savour the things of God**, **nor to have any evidence upon your soul for a better state hereafter**? (for indeed at that time all the things of God were hid from my soul).

334. Wherefore, when I at first began to think of this, it was a great trouble to me; for I thought with myself, that in the condition I now was in, I was not fit to die, neither indeed

did I think I could, if I should be called to it; besides, I thought with myself, if I should make a scrambling shift to clamber up the ladder, yet I should either with quaking, or other symptoms of fainting, give occasion to the enemy to reproach the way of God and His people for their timorousness. This, therefore, lay with great trouble upon me, for methought I was ashamed to die with a pale face, and tottering knees, in such a cause as this.

335. Wherefore I prayed to God that He would comfort me, and give me strength to do and suffer me what He should call me to; yet no comfort appeared, but all continued hid: I was also at this time, so really possessed with the thought of death, that oft I was as if I was on a ladder with the rope about my neck; only this was some encouragement to me; I thought I might now have an opportunity to speak my last words to a multitude, which I thought would come to see me die; and, thought I, if it must be so, if God will but

convert one soul by my very last words, I shall not count my life thrown away, nor lost.

336. But yet all the things of God were kept out of my sight, and still the tempter followed me with, **But whither must you go when you die**? **what will become of you**? **where will you be found in another world**? **what evidence have you for heaven and glory, and an inheritance among them that are sanctified**? Thus was I tossed for many weeks, and knew not what to do; at last this consideration fell with weight upon me, **that it was for the word and way of God that I was in this condition, Wherefore I was engaged not to flinch an hair's breadth from it**.

337. I thought also, that God might choose whether He would give me comfort now, or at the hour of death; but I might not therefore choose whether I would hold my profession or no: I was bound, but He was free; yea, 'twas my duty to stand to His word, whether He would ever look upon me

or save me at the last: wherefore, thought I, save the point being thus, I am for going on, and venturing my eternal state with Christ, whether I have comfort here or no; if God doth not come in, thought I, **I will leap off the ladder even blindfold into eternity, sink or swim, come heaven, come hell, Lord Jesus, if Thou wilt catch me, do**; if **not, I will venture for Thy name**.

338. I was no sooner fixed in this resolution, but the word dropped upon me, **Doth Job serve God for nought**? As if the accuser had said, **Lord, Job is no upright man, he serves Thee for bye-respects**: **hast Thou not made an hedge about him**, etc. **But put forth now Thine hand, and touch all that he hath, and, he will curse Thee to Thy face**. How now! thought I, is this the sign of an upright soul, to desire to serve God, when all is taken from him? Is he a godly man that will serve God for nothing, rather than give out! Blessed be God! then I hope I have an upright heart,

for I am resolved (God giving me strength) never to deny my profession, though I have nothing at all for my pains: and as I was thus considering, that scripture was set before me: Psalm xliv. 12, etc.

339. Now was my heart full of comfort; for I hoped it was sincere: I would not have been without this trial for much; I am comforted every time I think of it, and I hope I shall bless God for ever, for the teaching I have had by it. Many more of the dealings towards me I might relate, **But these out of the spoils won in battle I have dedicated to maintain the house of God**. 1 Chron. xxvi. 27.

The Conclusion

1. OF ALL THE TEMPTATIONS that ever I met with in my life, to question the being of God, and truth of His gospel is the worst, and the worst to be borne; when this temptation comes, it takes away my girdle from me, and removeth the foundation from under me: Oh! I have often thought of that word, **Have your loins girt about with truth**; and of that, **When the foundations are destroyed**, **what can the righteous do**?

2. Sometimes, when after sin committed, I have looked for sore chastisement from the hand of God, the very next that I have had from Him, hath been the discovery of His grace. Sometimes when I have been comforted, I have called myself a fool for my so sinking under trouble. And then again, when I have been cast down, I thought I was not wise, to give such way to comfort; with such strength and weight have both these been upon me.

3. I have wondered much at this one thing, that though God doth visit my soul with never so blessed a discovery of Himself, yet I have found again, that such hours have attended me afterwards, that I have been in my spirit so filled with darkness, that I could not so much as once conceive what that God and that comfort was, with which I have been refreshed.

4. I have sometimes seen more in a line of the Bible, than I could well tell how to stand under; and yet at another time, the

whole Bible hath been to me as dry as a stick; or rather, My heart hath been so dead and dry unto it, that I could not conceive the refreshment, though I have looked it all over.

5. Of all fears, they are best that are made by the blood of Christ; and of all joy, that is the sweetest that is mixed with mourning over Christ: Oh! it is a goodly thing to be on our knees, with Christ in our arms, before God: I hope I know something of these things.

6. I find to this day seven abominations in my heart: 1. Inclining to unbelief; 2. Suddenly to forget the love and mercy that Christ manifesteth; 3. A leaning to the works of the law; 4. Wanderings and coldness in prayer; 5. To forget to watch for that I pray for; 6. Apt to murmur because I have no more, and yet ready to abuse what I have; 7. I can do none of those things which God commands me, but my corruptions will thrust in themselves. When I would do good, evil is present with me.

7. These things I continually see and feel, and am afflicted and oppressed with, yet the wisdom of God doth order them for my good; 1. They make me abhor myself; 2. They keep me from trusting my heart; 3. They convince me of the insufficiency of all inherent righteousness; 4. They show me the necessity of flying to Jesus; 5. They press me to pray unto God; 6. They show me the need I have to watch and be sober; 7. And provoke me to pray unto God, through Christ, to help me, and carry me through this world.

A Relation of my Imprisonment in the Month of November 1660

WHEN, BY THE GOOD hand of my God, I had for five or six years together, without any interruption, freely preached the blessed gospel of our Lord Jesus Christ; and had also, through His blessed grace, some encouragement by His blessing thereupon; the devil, that old enemy of man's salvation, took his opportunity to inflame the hearts of his vassals against me, insomuch that at the last, I was laid out for by the warrant of a justice, and was taken and committed to prison. The relation thereof is as followeth: —

Upon the 12th of this instant, November 1660, I was desired by some of the friends in the country to come to teach at **Samsell**, by **Harlington**, in **Bedfordshire**. To whom I made a promise, if the Lord permitted, to be with them on the time aforesaid. The justice hearing thereof (whose name is Mr **Francis Wingate**), forthwith issued out his warrant to take me, and bring me before him, and in the meantime to keep a very strong watch about the house where the meeting should be kept, as if we that were to meet together in that place did intend to do some fearful business, to the destruction of the country; when alas! the constable, when he came in, found us only with our Bibles in our hands, ready to speak and hear the word of God; for we were just about to begin our exercise. Nay, we had begun in prayer for the blessing of God upon our opportunity, intending to have preached the word of the Lord unto them there present:[2] but the constable coming in prevented us. So I was taken and forced to depart the room. But had I been minded to have played the coward, I could have escaped and kept out of his hands. For when I was come to my friend's house, there was whispering that that day I should be taken, for there was a warrant out to take me; which when my friend heard, he being somewhat timorous, questioned whether we had best have our meeting or not; and whether it might not be better for me to depart, lest they should take me and have me before the justice, and after that send me to prison (for he knew better than I what spirit they were of, living by them): to whom I said, No, by no means, I will not stir, neither will I have the meeting

---

[2]   The text from which he intended to preach was, Doth thou believe on the Son of God? Jn. ix. 35. See Preface to his Confession of Faith.

dismissed for this. Come, be of good cheer; let us not be daunted; our cause is good, we need not be ashamed of it; to preach God's Word, is so good a work, that we shall be well rewarded, if we suffer for that; or to this purpose – (But as for my friend, I think he was more afraid of me, than of himself.) After this I walked into the close, where I somewhat seriously considering the matter, this came into my mind, That I had showed myself hearty and courageous in my preaching, and had, blessed be grace, made it my business to encourage others; therefore thought I, if I should now run, and make an escape, it will be of a very ill savour in the country. For what will my weak and newly-converted brethren think of it, but that I was not so strong in deed as I was in word? Also I feared that if I should run now there was a warrant out for me, I might by so doing make them afraid to stand, when great words only should be spoken to them. Besides I thought, that seeing God of His mercy should choose me to go upon the forlorn hope in this country; that is, to be the first, that should be opposed, for the gospel; if I should fly, it might be a discouragement to the whole body that might follow after. And further, I thought the world thereby would take occasion at my cowardliness, to have blasphemed the gospel, and to have had some ground to suspect worse of me and my profession, than I deserved. These things with others considered by me, I came in again to the house, with a full resolution to keep the meeting, and not to go away, though I could have been gone about an hour before the officer apprehended me; but I would not; for I was resolved to see the utmost of what they could say or do unto me. For blessed be the Lord, I knew of no evil that I had said or done. And so, as aforesaid, I begun the meeting. But being prevented by the constable's coming in with his warrant to take me, I could not proceed. But before I went away, I spake some few words of counsel and encouragement to the people, declaring to them, that they saw we were prevented of our opportunity to speak and hear the Word of God, and were like to suffer for the same; desiring them that they would not be discouraged, for it was a mercy to suffer upon so good account. For we might have been apprehended as thieves or murderers, or for other wickedness; but blessed be God it was not so, but we suffer as Christians for well doing: and we had better be the persecuted, than the persecutors, etc. But the constable and the justice's man waiting on us, would not be at quiet till they had me away and that we departed the house. But because the justice was not at home that day, there was a friend of mine engaged for me to bring me to the constable on the morrow morning. Otherwise the constable must have charged a watch with me, or have secured me some other way, my crime was so great. So on the next morning we went to the constable, and so to the justice.[3] He asked the constable what we did, where we was met together, and what we had with us? I trow, he meant whether we had armour or not; but when the constable told him that there were only met a few of us together to preach and hear the Word, and no sign of anything else, he could not well tell what to say: yet because he had sent for me, he did adventure to put out a few proposals to me, which were to this effect, namely, What I did there? And why I did not content myself with following my calling? for it was against the law, that such as I should be admitted to do as I did.

John Bunyan. To which I answered, That the intent of my coming thither, and to other places, was to instruct, and counsel people to forsake their sins, and close in with Christ, lest they did miserably perish; and that I could do both these without confusion (to wit), follow my calling, and preach the

---

[3]   Justice Wingate.

Word also.

At which words, he[4] was in a chafe, as it appeared; for he said that he would break the neck of our meetings.

Bun. I said, It may be so. Then he wished me to get sureties to be bound for me, or else he would send me to the jail.

My sureties being ready, I called them in, and when the bond for my appearance was made, he told them, that they was bound to keep me from preaching; and that if I did preach, their bonds would be forfeited. To which I answered, that then I should break them; for I should not leave speaking the Word of God: even to counsel, comfort, exhort, and teach the people among whom I came; and I thought this to be a work that had no hurt in it: but was rather worthy of commendation, than blame.

Wingate. Whereat he told me, that if they would not be so bound, my mittimus must

---

4   Ibid.

be made, and I sent to the jail, there to lie to the quarter sessions.

Now while my mittimus was making, the justice was withdrawn; and in comes an old enemy to the truth, Dr Lindale, who, when he was come in, fell to taunting at me with many reviling terms.

Bun. To whom I answered, that I did not come thither to talk with him, but with the justice. Whereat he supposed that I had nothing to say for myself, and triumphed as if he had got the victory; charging and condemning me for meddling with that for which I could show no warrant; and asked me, if I had taken the oaths? and if I had not, it was pity but that I should be sent to prison, etc.

I told him, that if I was minded, I could answer to any sober question that he should put to me. He then urged me again, how I could prove it lawful for me to preach, with a great deal of confidence of the victory.

But at last, because he should see that I

could answer him if I listed, I cited to him that verse in Peter, which saith, **every man hath received the gift, even so let him minister the same**, etc.

Lind. Aye, saith he, to whom is that spoken?

Bun. To whom, said I, why to every man that hath received a gift from God. Mark, saith the apostle, **As every man that hath received a gift from God**, etc.; and again, **You may all prophesy one by one**. Whereat the man was a little stopt, and went a softlier pace: but not being willing to lose the day, he began again, and said: –

Lind. Indeed, I do remember that I have read of one Alexander a coppersmith, who did much oppose, and disturb the apostles; – (aiming it is like at me, because I was a tinker).

Bun. To which I answered, that I also had read of very many priests and pharisees, that had their hands in the blood of our Lord Jesus Christ.

Lind. Aye, saith he, and you are one of those scribes and pharisees: for you, with a pretence, make long prayers to devour widows' houses.

Bun. I answered, that if he had got no more by preaching and praying than I had done, he would not be so rich as now he was. But that scripture coming into my mind, **Answer not a fool according to his folly**, I was as sparing of my speech as I could, without prejudice to truth.

Now by this time my mittimus was made, and I committed to the constable, to be sent to the jail in Bedford, etc.

But as I was going, two of my brethren met with me by the way, and desired the constable to stay, supposing that they should prevail with the justice, through the favour of a pretended friend, to let me go at liberty. So we did stay, while they went to the justice; and after much discourse with him, it came to this: that if I would come to him again, and say some certain words to him, I should be released. Which when they told me, I said if the words was such that might be said with a good conscience, I should or else I should not. So through their importunity went back again, but not believing that I should be delivered: for I feared their spirit was too full of opposition to the truth to let me go, unless I should, in something or other, dishonour my God and wound my conscience. Wherefore, as I went, I lifted up my heart to God, for light and strength to be kept, that I might not do any thing that might either dishonour Him, or wrong my own soul, or be a grief or discouragement to any that was inclining after the Lord Jesus Christ.

Well, when I came to the justice again, there was Mr **Foster** of Bedford, who, coming out of another room, and seeing me by the light of the candle (for it was dark night when I went thither), he said unto me, Who is there? **John Bunyan**? with such seeming affection, as if he would have leaped on my neck and kissed[5] me, which made me somewhat wonder, that such a man as he, with whom I had so little acquaintance, and, besides, that had ever been a close opposer of the ways of God, should carry himself so full of love to me; but, afterwards, when I saw what he did, it caused me to remember those sayings, **Their tongues are smoother than oil, but their words are drawn swords**. And again, **Beware of men, etc.** When I[6] had answered him, that blessed be God, I was well; he said, What is the occasion of your being here? or to that purpose. To whom I answered, that I was at a meeting of people a little way off, intending to speak a word of exhortation to them; the justice hearing thereof, said I, was pleased to send his warrant to fetch me before him, etc.

Fost. So (said he), I understand: but well, if you will promise to call the people no more

---

5   A right Judas.
6   Bunyan.

together, you shall have your liberty to go home; for my brother is very loath to send you to prison, if you will be but ruled.

Bun. Sir (said I), pray what do you mean by calling the people together? my business is not anything among them, when they are come together, but to exhort them to look after the salvation of their souls, that they may be saved, etc.

Fost. Saith he, We must not enter into explication, or dispute now; but if you will say you will call the people no more together, you may have your liberty; if not, you must be sent away to prison.

Bun. Sir, said I, I shall not force or compel any man to hear me; but yet, if I come into any place where there is a people met together, I should, according to the best of my skill and wisdom, exhort and counsel them to seek out after the Lord Jesus Christ, for the salvation of their souls.

Fost. He said, That was none of my work; I must follow my calling; and if I would but leave off preaching, and follow my calling, I should have the justice's favour, and be acquitted presently.

Bun. To whom I said, that I could follow my calling, and that too, namely, preaching the Word: and I did look upon it as my duty to do them both, as I had an opportunity.

Fost. He said, To have any such meetings was against the law; and, therefore, he would have me leave off, and say, I would call the people no more together.

Bun. To whom I said, that I durst not make any further promise; for my conscience would not suffer me to do it. And again, I did look upon it as my duty to do as much good as I could, not only in my trade, but also in communicating to all people wheresoever I came the best knowledge I had in the Word.

Fost. He told me that I was the nearest the Papists of any, and that he would convince me of immediately.

Bun. I asked him, Wherein?

Fost. He said, In that we understood the

Scriptures literally.

Bun. I told him that those that were to be understood literally, we understood them so; but for those that was to be understood otherwise, we endeavoured so to understand them.

Fost. He said, Which of the Scriptures do you understand literally?

Bun. I said this, **He that believes shall be saved**. This was to be understood just as it is spoken; that whosoever believeth in Christ shall, according to the plain and simple words of the text, be saved.

Fost. He said that I was ignorant, and did not understand the Scriptures; for how, said he, can you understand them when you know not the original Greek? etc.

Bun. To whom I said, that if that was his opinion, that none could understand the Scriptures but those that had the original Greek, etc., then but a very few of the poorest sort should be saved (this is harsh); yet the Scripture saith, **That God hides**

these things from the wise and prudent (that is, from the learned of the world), **and reveals them to babes and sucklings**.

Fost. He said there were none that heard me but a company of foolish people.

Bun. I told him that there was the wise as well as the foolish that do hear me; and again, those that were most commonly counted foolish by the world are the wisest before God; also, that God had rejected the wise, and mighty, and noble, and chosen the foolish, and the base.

Fost. He told me that I made people neglect their calling; and that God had commanded people to work six days, and serve Him on the seventh.

Bun. I told him that it was the duty of people, (both rich and poor), to look out for their souls on them days as well as for their bodies; and that God would have His people exhort one another daily, while it is called to-day.

Fost. He said again that there were none

but a company of poor, simple, ignorant people that come to hear me.

Bun. I told him that the foolish and the ignorant had most need of teaching and information; and, therefore, it would be profitable for me to go on in that work.

Fost. Well, said he, to conclude, but will you promise that you will not call the people together any more? and then you may be released and go home.

Bun. I told him that I durst say no more than I had said; for I durst not leave off that work which God had called me to.

So he withdrew from me, and then came several of the justice's servants to me, and told me that I stood so much upon a nicety. Their master, they said, was willing to let me go; and if I would but say I would call the people no more together, I might have my liberty, etc.

Bun. I told them there were more ways than one in which a man might be said to call the people together. As for instance, if a man get upon the market-place, and there read a book, or the like, though he do not say to the people, Sirs, come hither and hear; yet if they come to him because he reads, he, by his very reading, may be said to call them together; because they would not have been there to hear if he had not been there to read. And seeing this might be termed a calling the people together; I durst not say, I would not call them together; for then, by the same argument, my preaching might be said to call them together.

Wing. and Fost. Then came the justice and Mr Foster to me again; (we had a little more discourse about preaching, but because the method of it is out of my mind, I pass it); and when they saw that I was at a point, and would not be moved nor persuaded, Mr Foster, the man that did at first express so much love to me, told the justice that then he must send me away to prison. And that he would do well, also, if he would present all those that were the cause of my coming among them to meetings. Thus we parted.

And, verily, as I was going forth of the doors, I had much ado to forbear saying to them that I carried the peace of God along with me; but I held my peace, and, blessed be the Lord, went away to prison, with God's comfort in my poor soul.

After I had lain in the jail five or six days, the brethren sought means, again, to get me out by bondsmen; (for so ran my mittimus, that I should lie there till I could find sureties). They went to a justice at Elstow, one Mr Crumpton, to desire him to take bond for my appearing at the quarter sessions. At the first he told them he would; but afterwards he made a demur at the business, and desired first to see my mittimus, which ran to this purpose: That I went about to several conventicles in the county, to the great disparagement of the government of the church of England, etc. When he had seen it, he said that there might be something more against me than was expressed in my mittimus; and that he was but a young man, therefore he durst not do it. This my jailor told me; and, whereat I was not at all daunted but rather glad, and saw evidently that the Lord had heard me; for before I went down to the justice, I begged of God that if I might do more good by being at liberty than in prison, that then I might be set at liberty; but if not, His will be done; for I was not altogether without hopes but that my imprisonment might be an awakening to the saints in the country, therefore I could not tell well which to choose; only I, in that manner, did commit the thing to God. And verily, at my return, I did meet my God sweetly in the prison again, comforting of me and satisfying of me that it was His will and mind that I should be there.

When I came back again to prison, as I was musing at the slender answer of the justice, this word dropt in upon my heart with some life, **For He knew that for envy they had delivered Him**.

Thus have I, in short, declared the manner and occasion of my being in prison; where I lie waiting the good will of God, to do with me as He pleaseth; knowing that not one hair of my head can fall to the ground without the will of my Father, which is in heaven. Let the rage and malice of men be never so great, they can do no more, nor go any further, than God permits them; but when they have done their worst, We know all things shall work together for good to them that love God.

Farewell.

Here is the Sum of my Examination before Justice Keelin, **Justice** Chester, **Justice** Blundale, **Justice** Beecher, **Justice** Snagg, **etc.**

After I had lain in prison above seven weeks, the quarter-sessions were to be kept in Bedford, for the county thereof, unto which

I was to be brought; and when my jailor had set me before those justices, there was a bill of indictment preferred against me. The extent thereof was as followeth: That John Bunyan, of the town of Bedford, labourer, being a person of such and such conditions, he hath (since such a time) devilishly and perniciously abstained from coming to church to hear Divine service, and is a common upholder of several unlawful meetings and conventicles, to the great disturbance and distraction of the good subjects of this kingdom, contrary to the laws of our sovereign lord the King, etc.

The Clerk. When this was read, the clerk of the sessions said unto me, What say you to this?

Bun. I said, that as to the first part of it, I was a common frequenter of the Church of God. And was also, by grace, a member with the people, over whom Christ is the Head.

Keelin. But, saith Justice **Keelin** (who

was the judge in that court), do you come to church (you know what I mean); to the parish church, to hear Divine service?

Bun. I answered, No, I did not.

Keel. He asked me, Why?

Bun. I said, Because I did not find it commanded in the Word of God.

Keel. He said, We were commanded to pray.

Bun. I said, But not by the Common Prayer-Book.

Keel. He said, How then?

Bun. I said, With the Spirit. As the apostle saith, **I will pray with the Spirit**, **and with the understanding**. 1 Cor. xiv. 15.

Keel. He said, We might pray with the Spirit, and with the understanding, and with the Common Prayer-Book also.

Bun. I said, that the prayers in the Common Prayer-Book were such as was made by other men, and not by the motions of the Holy Ghost, within our hearts; and as I said, the apostle saith, he will pray with the Spirit, and with the understanding; not with the Spirit and the Common Prayer-Book.

Another Justice. What do you count prayer? Do you think it is to say a few words over before or among a people?

Bun. I said, No, not so; for men might have many elegant, or excellent words, and yet not pray at all; but when a man prayeth, he doth, through a sense of those things which he wants (which sense is begotten by the Spirit), pour out his heart before God through Christ; though his words be not so many and so excellent as others are.

Justices. They said, That was true.

Bun. I said, This might be done without the Common Prayer-Book.

Another. One of them said (I think it was Justice **Blundale**, or Justice **Snagg**), How should we know that you do not write out your prayers first, and then read them afterwards to the people? This he spake in a laughing way.

Bun. I said, it is not our use, to take a pen and paper, and write a few words thereon, and then go and read it over to a company of people.

But how should we know it, said he?

Bun. Sir, it is none of our custom, said I.

Keel. But said Justice **Keelin**, It is lawful to use the Common Prayer, and such like forms: for Christ taught His disciples to pray, as John also taught his disciples. And further, said he, Cannot one man teach another to pray? Faith comes by hearing; and one man may convince another of sin, and therefore prayers made by men, and read over, are good to teach, and help men to pray.

While he was speaking these words, God brought that word into my mind, in the eighth of the Romans, at the 26th verse. I say, God brought it, for I thought not on it before: but as he was speaking, it came so fresh into my mind, and was set so evidently before me, as if the scripture had said, Take me, take me; so when he had done speaking,

Bun. I said, Sir, the scripture saith, that **it is the spirit that helpeth our infirmities**; for we know not what we should pray for as we ought: but the Spirit itself maketh intercession for us, with sighs and groanings which cannot be uttered. Mark, said I, it doth not say the Common Prayer-Book teacheth us how to pray, but the Spirit. And it is **the Spirit that helpeth our infirmities**, saith the apostle; he doth not say it is the Common Prayer-Book.

And as to the Lord's prayer, although it be an easy thing to say, **Our Father**, etc., with the mouth; yet there is very few that can, in the Spirit, say the two first words in that prayer; that is, that can call God their Father, as knowing what it is to be born again, and as having experience, that they are begotten of the Spirit of God: which if they do not, all is but babbling, etc.

Keel. Justice **Keelin** said that that was a truth.

Bun. And I say further, as to your saying that one man may convince another of sin, and that faith comes by hearing, and that one man may tell another how he should pray, etc., I say men may tell each other of their sins, but it is the Spirit that must convince them.

And though it be said that **faith comes by hearing**: yet it is the Spirit that worketh faith in the heart through hearing, or else **they are not profited by hearing**. Heb. iv. 12.

And that though one man may tell another how he should pray: yet, as I said before, he cannot pray, nor make his condition known to God, except the Spirit help. It is not the Common Prayer-Book that can do this. It is the **Spirit that showeth us our sins**, and the **Spirit that showeth us a Saviour**, Jn. xvi. 16, and the Spirit that stirreth up in our hearts desires to come to God, for such things as we stand in need of, Matt. xi. 27, even sighing out our souls unto Him for them with **groans which**

cannot be uttered. With other words to the same purpose. At this they were set.

Keel. But says Justice **Keelin**, What have you against the Common Prayer-Book?

Bun. I said, Sir, if you will hear me, I shall lay down my reasons against it.

Keel. He said I should have liberty; but first, said he, let me give you one caution; take heed of speaking irreverently of the Common Prayer-Book; for if you do so, you will bring great damage upon yourself.

Bun. So I proceeded, and said, My first reason was, because it was not commanded in the Word of God, and therefore I could not use it.

Another. One of them said, Where do you find it commanded in the Scripture, that you should go to **Elstow**, or **Bedford**, and yet it is lawful to go to either of them, is it not?

Bun. I said, To go to **Elstow**, or **Bedford**, was a civil thing, and not material, though not commanded, and yet God's Word allowed me to go about my calling, and therefore if it lay there, then to go thither, etc. But to pray, was a great part of the Divine worship of God, and therefore it ought to be done according to the rule of God's Word.

Another. One of them said, He will do harm; let him speak no further.

Keel. Justice **Keelin** said, No, no, never fear him, we are better established than so; he can do no harm; we know the Common Prayer-Book hath been ever since the apostles' time, and it is lawful for it to be used in the church.

Bun. I said, Show me the place in the epistles, where the Common Prayer-Book is written, or one text of Scripture, that commands me to read it, and I will use it. But yet, notwithstanding, said I, they that have a mind to use it, they have their liberty; that is, I would not keep them from it; but for our parts, we can pray to God without it. Blessed be His name!

With that, one of them said, Who is your God? Beelzebub? Moreover, they often said, that I was possessed with the spirit of delusion, and of the devil. All which sayings I passed over; the Lord forgive them! And further, I said, Blessed be the Lord for it; we are encouraged to meet together, and to pray, and exhort one another; for, we have had the comfortable presence of God among us. For ever blessed be His holy name!

Keel. Justice **Keelin** called this pedler's French, saying, that I must leave off my canting. The Lord open his eyes!

Bun. I said that we ought to exhort one another daily, while it is called to-day, etc.

Keel. Justice **Keelin** said that I ought not to preach; and asked me where I had my authority? with other such like words.

Bun. I said that I would prove that it was lawful for me, and such as I am, to preach the Word of God.

Keel. He said unto me, By what Scripture?

Bun. I said, By that in the first epistle of Peter, chap. iv. 10, 11, and Acts xviii., with other Scriptures, which he would not suffer me to mention. But said, Hold; not so many, which is the first?

Bun. I said this: **As every man hath received the gift, even so let him minister the same unto another, as good stewards of the manifold grace of God. If any man speak, let him speak as the oracles of God, etc.**

Keel. He said, Let me a little open that Scripture to you: **As every man hath received the gift**; that is, said he, as every one hath received a trade, so let him follow it. If any man have received a gift of tinkering, as thou hast done, let him follow his tinkering. And so other men their trades. And the divine his calling, etc.

Bun. Nay, sir, said I, but it is most clear, that the apostle speaks here of preaching the Word; if you do but compare both the verses together, the next verse explains this gift what it is, saying, **if any man speak, let him speak as the oracles of God.** So that it is plain, that the Holy Ghost doth not so much in this place exhort to civil callings, as to the exercising of those gifts that we have received from God. I would have gone on, but he would not give me leave.

Keel. He said, We might do it in our families, but not otherways.

Bun. I said, If it was lawful to do good to some, it was lawful to do good to more. If it was a good duty to exhort our families, it was good to exhort others; but if they held it a sin to meet together to seek the face of God, and exhort one another to follow Christ, I should sin still; for so we should do.

Keel. He said he was not so well versed in Scripture as to dispute, or words to that purpose. And said, moreover, that they could not wait upon me any longer; but said to me, Then you confess the indictment, do you not? Now, and not till now, I saw I was indicted.

Bun. I said, This I confess, we have had

many meetings together, both to pray to God, and to exhort one another, and that we had the sweet comforting presence of the Lord among us for our encouragement; blessed be His name therefore. I confessed myself guilty no otherwise.

Keel. Then, said he, bear your judgment. You must be had back again to prison, and there lie for three months following; and at three months' end, if you do not submit to go to church to hear Divine service, and leave your preaching, you must be banished the realm: and if, after such a day as shall be appointed you to be gone, you shall be found in this realm, etc., or be found to come over again without special licence from the king, etc., you must stretch by the neck for it, I tell you plainly: and so he bid my jailor have me away.

Bun. I told him, as to this matter, I was at a point with him; for if I were out of prison to-day, I would preach the Gospel again to-morrow, by the help of God.

Another. To which one made me some answer: but my jailor pulling me away to be gone, I could not tell what he said.

Thus I departed from them; and I can truly say, I bless the Lord **Jesus Christ** for it, that my heart was sweetly refreshed in the time of my examination, and also afterwards, at my returning to the prison. So that I found Christ's words more than bare trifles, where He saith, **I will give you a mouth and wisdom**, **which all your adversaries shall not be able to gainsay**, **nor resist**. Luke xxi. 15. And that His peace no man can take from us.

Thus have I given you the substance of my examination. The Lord make this profitable to all that shall read or hear it. Farewell.

The Substance of some Discourse had between the Clerk of the Peace and myself; **when he came to admonish me**, **according to the tenor of that Law**, **by which I was in prison**.

When I had lain in prison other twelve weeks, and now not knowing what they intended to do with me, upon the third of April 1661, comes Mr Cobb unto me (as he told me), being sent by the justices to admonish me; and demand of me submittance to the church of England, etc. The extent of our discourse was as followeth.

Cobb. When he was come into the house he sent for me out of my chamber; who, when I was come unto him, he said, Neighbour **Bunyan**, how do you do?

Bun. I thank you, Sir, said I, very well, blessed be the Lord.

Cobb. Saith he, I come to tell you, that it is desired you would submit yourself to the laws of the land, or else at the next sessions it will go worse with you, even to be sent away out of the nation, or else worse than that.

Bun. I said that I did desire to demean myself in the world, both as becometh a man and a Christian.

Cobb. But, saith he, you must submit to the laws of the land, and leave off those meetings which you was wont to have; for the statute-law is directly against it; and I am sent to you by the justices to tell you that they do intend to prosecute the law against you if you submit not.

Bun. I said, Sir, I conceive that that law by which I am in prison at this time, doth not reach or condemn either me, or the meetings which I do frequent; that law was made against those, that being designed to do evil in their meetings, making the exercise of religion their pretence, to cover their wickedness. It doth not forbid the private meetings of those that plainly and simply make it their only end to worship the Lord, and to exhort one another to edification. My end in meeting with others is simply to do as much good as I can, by exhortation and counsel, according to that small measure of light which God hath given me, and not to disturb the peace of the nation.

Cobb. Every one will say the same, said he; you see the late insurrection[7] at **London**, under what glorious pretences they went; and yet, indeed, they intended no less than the ruin of the kingdom and commonwealth.

Bun. That practice of theirs, I abhor, said I; yet it doth not follow that, because they did so, therefore all others will do so. I look upon it as my duty to behave myself under the King's government, both as becomes a man and a Christian, and if an occasion were offered me, I should willingly manifest my loyalty to my Prince, both by word and deed.

Cobb. Well, said he, I do not profess myself to be a man that can dispute; but this I say, truly, neighbour **Bunyan**, I would have you consider this matter seriously, and submit yourself; you may have your

---

7   The Venner insurrection is here referred to.

liberty to exhort your neighbour in private discourse, so be you do not call together an assembly of people; and, truly, you may do much good to the church of Christ, if you would go this way; and this you may do, and the law not abridge you of it. It is your private meetings that the law is against.

Bun. Sir, said I, if I may do good to one by my discourse? why may I not do good to two? And if to two, why not to four, and so to eight? etc.

Cobb. Ay, saith he, and to a hundred, I warrant you.

Bun. Yes, Sir, said I, I think I should not be forbid to do as much good as I can.

Cobb. But, saith he, you may but pretend to do good, and instead, notwithstanding, do harm, by seducing the people; you are, therefore, denied your meeting so many together, lest you should do harm.

Bun. And yet, said I, you say the law tolerates me to discourse with my neighbour; surely there is no law tolerates me seduce any one; therefore if I may by the law discourse with one, surely it is to do him good; and if I by discoursing may do good to one, surely, by the same law, I may do good to many.

Cobb. The law, saith he, doth expressly forbid your private meetings; therefore they are not to be tolerated.

Bun. I told him that I would not entertain so much uncharitableness of that Parliament in the 35th of **Elizabeth**, or of the Queen herself, as to think they did, by that law, intend the oppressing of any of God's ordinances, or the interrupting any in way of God; but men may, in the wresting of it, turn it against the way of God; but take the law in itself, and it only fighteth against those that drive at mischief in their hearts and meeting, making religion only their cloak, colour, or pretence; for so are the words of the statute: **If any meetings, under colour or pretence of religion, etc.**

Cobb. Very good; therefore the king, seeing that pretences are usually in and among people, so as to make religion their pretence only; therefore he, and the law before him, doth forbid such private meetings, and tolerates only public; you may meet in public.

Bun. Sir, said I, let me answer you in a similitude: Set the case that, at such a wood corner, there did usually come forth thieves, to do mischief; must there therefore a law be made, that every one that cometh out there shall be killed? May not there come out true men as well as thieves out from thence? Just thus is it in this case; I do think there may be many that may design the destruction of the commonwealth; but it doth not follow therefore that all private meetings are unlawful; those that transgress, let them be punished. And if at any time I myself should do any act in my conversation as doth not become a man and Christian, let me bear the punishment. And as for your saying I may meet in public, if I may be suffered, I would gladly do it. Let me have but meeting enough in public, and I shall care the less to have them in private. I do not meet in private because I am afraid to have meetings in public. I bless the Lord that my heart is at that point, that if any man can lay any thing to my charge, either in doctrine or in practice, in this particular, that can be proved error or heresy, I am willing to disown it, even in the very market-place; but if it be truth, then to stand to it to the last drop of my blood. And, Sir, said I, you ought to commend me for so doing. To err and to be a heretic are two things; I am no heretic, because I will not stand refractorily to defend any one thing that is contrary to the Word. Prove any thing which I hold to be an error, and I will recant it.

Cobb. But, goodman **Bunyan**, said he, methinks you need not stand so strictly upon this one thing, as to have meetings of such public assemblies. Cannot you submit, and, notwithstanding, do as much good as you can, in a neighbourly way, without having such meetings?

Bun. Truly, Sir, said I, I do not desire to commend myself, but to think meanly of myself; yet when I do most despise myself, taking notice of that small measure of light which God hath given me, also that the people of the Lord (by their own saying), are edified thereby. Besides, when I see that the Lord, through grace, hath in some measure blessed my labour, I dare not but exercise that gift which God hath given me for the good of the people. And I said further, that I would willingly speak in public if I might.

Cobb. He said, that I might come to the public assemblies and hear. What though you do not preach? you may hear. Do not think yourself so well enlightened, and that you have received a gift so far above others, but that you may hear other men preach. Or to that purpose.

Bun. I told him, I was as willing to be taught as to give instruction, and I looked upon it as my duty to do both; for, said I, a man that is a teacher, he himself may learn also from another that teacheth, as the apostle saith, **We may all prophesy one by one**, **that all may learn**. 1 Cor. xiv. 31. That is, every man that hath received a gift from God, he may dispense it, that others may be comforted; and when he hath done, he may hear and learn, and be comforted himself of others.

Cobb. But, said he, what if you should forbear awhile, and sit still, till you see further how things will go?

Bun. Sir, said I, **Wickliffe** saith, that he which leaveth off preaching and hearing of the Word of God for fear of excommunication of men, he is already excommunicated of God, and shall in the day of judgment be counted a traitor to Christ.[8]

Cobb. Ay, saith he, they that do not hear shall be so counted indeed; do you,

---

[8]   Bunyan here refers to a translation of Wickliffe's doctrine in John Foxe's Martyrology, a favourite book of his.

therefore, hear?

Bun. But, Sir, said I, he saith, he that shall leave off either preaching or hearing, etc. That is, if he hath received a gift for edification, it is his sin, if he doth not lay it out in a way of exhortation and counsel, according to the proportion of his gift; as well as to spend his time altogether in hearing others preach.

Cobb. But, said he, how shall we know that you have received a gift?

Bun. Said I, Let any man hear and search, and prove the doctrine by the Bible.

Cobb. But will you be willing, said he, that two indifferent persons shall determine the case; and will you stand by their judgment?

Bun. I said, Are they infallible?

Cobb. He said, No.

Bun. Then, said I, it is possible my judgment may be as good as theirs. But yet I will pass by either, and in this matter be judged by the Scriptures; I am sure that is infallible, and cannot err.

Cobb. But, said he, who shall be judge between you, for you take the Scriptures one way, and they another?

Bun. I said the Scripture should: and that by comparing one Scripture with another; for that will open itself, if it be rightly compared. As for instance, if under the different apprehensions of the word **Mediator**, you would know the truth of it, the Scriptures open it, and tell us that he that is a mediator must take up the business between two, and a mediator is not a mediator of one, – **but God is one**, **and there is one Mediator between God and men**, **even the man Christ Jesus**. Gal. iii. 20; 1 Tim. ii. 5. So likewise the Scripture calleth Christ a **complete**, or perfect, or able **high priest**. That is opened in that He is called man, and also God. His blood also is discovered to be effectually efficacious by the same things. So the Scripture, as touching the matter of meeting together, etc., doth likewise sufficiently open itself and discover its meaning.

Cobb. But are you willing, said he, to stand to the judgment of the church?

Bun. Yes, Sir, said I, to the approbation of the church of God; (the church's judgment is best expressed in Scripture). We had much other discourse which I cannot well remember, about the laws of the nation, and submission to governments; to which I did tell him, that I did look upon myself as bound in conscience to walk according to all righteous laws, and that, whether there was a king or no; and if I did any thing that was contrary, I did hold it my duty to bear patiently the penalty of the law, that was provided against such offenders; with many more words to the like effect. And said, moreover, that to cut off all occasions of suspicion from any, as touching the harmlessness of my doctrine in private, I would willingly take the pains to give any one the notes of all my sermons; for I do sincerely desire to live quietly in my country, and to submit to the present authority.

Cobb. Well, neighbour **Bunyan**, said he, but indeed I would wish you seriously to consider of these things, between this and the quarter-sessions, and to submit yourself. You may do much good if you continue still in the land; but alas, what benefit will it be to your friends, or what good can you do to them, if you should be sent away beyond the seas into **Spain**, or **Constantinople**, or some other remote part of the world? Pray be ruled.

Jailor. Indeed, Sir, I hope he will be ruled.

Bun. I shall desire, said I, in all honesty to behave myself in the nation, whilst I am in it. And if I must be so dealt withal, as you say, I hope God will help me to bear what they shall lay upon me. I know no evil that I have done in this matter, to be so used. I speak as in the presence of God.

Cobb. You know, saith he, that the Scripture saith, **the powers that be**, **are ordained of God**.

Bun. I said, Yes, and that I was to submit

to the King as supreme, and also to the governors, as to them who are sent by Him.

Cobb. Well then, said he, the King then commands you, that you should not have any private meetings; because it is against his law, and he is ordained of God, therefore you should not have any.

Bun. I told him that **Paul** did own the powers that were in his day, to be of God; and yet he was often in prison under them for all that. And also, though **Jesus Christ** told **Pilate**, that He had no power against him, but of God, yet He died under the same **Pilate**; and yet, said I, I hope you will not say that either **Paul**, or Christ, were such as did deny magistracy, and so sinned against God in slighting the ordinance. Sir, said I, the law hath provided two ways of obeying: the one to do that which I, in my conscience, do believe that I am bound to do, actively; and where I cannot obey actively, there I am willing to lie down, and to suffer what they shall do unto me. At this he sat still, and said no more; which when he had done, I did thank him for his civil and meek discoursing with me; and so we parted.

O! that we might meet in heaven!

Farewell. J. B.

Here followeth a discourse between my Wife and the Judges, with others, touching my Deliverance at the Assizes following; the which I took from her own Mouth.

After that I had received this sentence of banishing, or hanging, from them, and after the former admonition, touching the determination of the justices if I did not recant; just when the time drew nigh, in which I should have abjured, or have done worse (as Mr Cobb told me), came the time in which the King was to be crowned.[9] Now, at the coronation of kings, there is usually a releasement of divers prisoners, by

---

[9]   April 23, 1661.

virtue of his coronation; in which privilege also I should have had my share; but that they took me for a convicted person, and therefore, unless I sued out a pardon (as they called it), I could have no benefit thereby, notwithstanding, yet, forasmuch as the coronation proclamation did give liberty, from the day the King was crowned, to that day twelvemonth, to sue them out; therefore, though they would not let me out of prison, as they let out thousands, yet they could not meddle with me, as touching the execution of their sentence; because of the liberty offered for the suing out of pardons. Whereupon I continued in prison till the next assizes, which are called **Midsummer assizes**, being then kept in **August**, 1661.

Now, at that assizes, because I would not leave any possible means unattempted that might be lawful, I did, by my wife, present a petition to the judges three times, that I might be heard, and that they would impartially take my case into consideration.

The first time my wife went, she presented it to Judge **Hale**, who very mildly received it at her hand, telling her that he would do her and me the best good he could; but he feared, he said, he could do none. The next day, again, lest they should, through the multitude of business, forget me, we did throw another petition into the coach to Judge **Twisdon**; who, when he had seen it, snapt her up, and angrily told her that I was a convicted person, and could not be released, unless I would promise to preach no more, etc.

Well, after this, she yet again presented another to judge Hale, as he sat on the bench, who, as it seemed, was willing to give her audience. Only Justice **Chester** being present, stept up and said, that I was convicted in the court, and that I was a hot-spirited fellow (or words to that purpose), whereat he waived it, and did not meddle therewith. But yet, my wife being encouraged by the high-sheriff, did venture once more into their presence (as the poor widow did before the unjust judge) to try what she could do with them for my liberty, before they went forth of the town. The place where she went to them, was to the **Swan-chamber**, where the two judges, and many justices and gentry of the country, was in company together. She then coming into the chamber with a bashed face, and a trembling heart, began her errand to them in this manner: –

Woman. My lord (directing herself to judge Hale), I make bold to come once again to your Lordship, to know what may be done with my husband.

Judge Hale. To whom he said, Woman, I told thee before I could do thee no good; because they have taken that for a conviction which thy husband spoke at the sessions: and unless there be something done to undo that, I can do thee no good.

Woman. My lord, said she, he is kept

unlawfully in prison; they clapped him up before there was any proclamation against the meetings; the indictment also is false. Besides, they never asked him whether he was guilty or no; neither did he confess the indictment.

One of the Justices. Then one of the justices that stood by, whom she knew not, said, My Lord, he was lawfully convicted.

Wom. It is false, said she; for when they said to him, Do you confess the indictment? he said only this, that he had been at several meetings, both where there were preaching the Word, and prayer, and that they had God's presence among them.

Judge Twisdon. Whereat Judge **Twisdon** answered very angrily, saying, What, you think we can do what we list; your husband is a breaker of the peace, and is convicted by the law, etc. Whereupon Judge **Hale** called for the Statute Book.

Wom. But, said she, my lord, he was not lawfully convicted.

Chester. Then Justice **Chester** said, My lord, he was lawfully convicted.

Wom. It is false, said she; it was but a word of discourse that they took for a conviction (as you heard before).

Chest. But it is recorded, woman; it is recorded, said Justice **Chester**; as if it must be of necessity true, because it was recorded. With which words he often endeavoured to stop her mouth, having no other argument to convince her, but it is recorded, it is recorded.

Wom. My Lord, said she, I was a while since at **London**, to see if I could get my husband's liberty; and there I spoke with my lord **Barkwood**, one of the House of Lords, to whom I delivered a petition, who took it of me and presented it to some of the rest of the House of Lords, for my husband's releasement; who, when they had seen it, they said, that they could not release him, but had committed his releasement to the judges, at the next assizes. This he told me; and now I am come to you to see if any thing may be done in this business, and you give neither releasement nor relief. To which they gave her no answer, but made as if they heard her not.

Chest. Only Justice **Chester** was often up with this, – He is convicted, and it is recorded.

Wom. If it be, it is false, said she.

Chest. My lord, said Justice **Chester**, he is a pestilent fellow, there is not such a fellow in the country again.

Twis. What, will your husband leave preaching? If he will do so, then send for him.

Wom. My lord, said she, he dares not leave preaching as long as he can speak.

Twis. See here, what should we talk any more about such a fellow? Must he do what he lists? He is a breaker of the peace.

Wom. She told him again, that he desired to live peaceably, and to follow his calling, that his family might be maintained; and moreover, said, My Lord, I have four small children, that cannot help themselves, one of which is blind, and have nothing to live upon, but the charity of good people.

Hale. Hast thou four children? said Judge Hale; thou art but a young woman to have four children.

Wom. My lord, said she, I am but mother-in-law to them, having not been married to him yet full two years. Indeed, I was with child when my husband was first apprehended; but being young, and unaccustomed to such things, said she, I being smayed[10] at the news, fell into labour, and so continued for eight days, and then was delivered, but my child died.

Hale. Whereat, he looking very soberly on the matter, said, Alas, poor woman!

Twis. But Judge **Twisdon** told her, that she made poverty her cloak; and said, moreover, that he understood I was maintained better by running up and down a preaching, than

---

[10] 'Smayed,' an obsolete contraction of 'dismayed,'

by following my calling.

Hale. What is his calling? said Judge Hale.

Answer. Then some of the company that stood by, said, A tinker, my lord.

Wom. Yes, said she; and because he is a tinker, and a poor man, therefore he is despised, and cannot have justice.

Hale. Then Judge **Hale** answered very mildly, saying, I tell thee, woman, seeing it is so, that they have taken what thy husband spake for a conviction; thou must either apply thyself to the King, or sue out his pardon, or get a writ of error.

Chest. But when Justice **Chester** heard him give her this counsel; and especially (as she supposed) because he spoke of a writ of error, he chafed, and seemed to be very much offended; saying, My lord, he will preach and do what he lists.

Wom. He preacheth nothing but the Word of God, said she.

Twis. He preach the Word of God! said Twisdon; and withal, she thought he would have struck her; he runneth up and down, and doth harm.

Wom. No, my lord, said she, it is not so; God hath owned him, and done much good by him.

Twis. God! said he, his doctrine is the doctrine of the devil.

Wom. My lord, said she, when the righteous Judge shall appear, it will be known that his doctrine is not the doctrine of the devil.

Twis. My lord, said he, to Judge Hale, do not mind her, but send her away.

Hale. Then said Judge Hale, I am sorry, woman, that I can do thee no good; thou must do one of those three things aforesaid, namely, either to apply thyself to the King, or sue out his pardon, or get a writ of error; but a writ of error will be cheapest.

Wom. At which Chester again seemed to be in a chafe, and put off his hat, and as she thought, scratched his head for anger: but when I saw, said she, that there was no prevailing to have my husband sent for, though I often desired them that they would send for him, that he might speak for himself; telling them, that he could give them better satisfaction than I could, in what they demanded of him, with several other things, which now I forget; only this I remember, that though I was somewhat timorous at my first entrance into the chamber, yet before I went out, I could not but break forth into tears, not so much because they were so hard-hearted against me, and my husband, but to think what a sad account such poor creatures will have to give at the coming of the Lord, when they shall there answer for all things whatsoever they have done in the body, whether it be good, or whether it be bad.

So, when I departed from them, the book of statutes was brought, but what they said of it I know nothing at all, neither did I hear any more from them.

Some Carriages of the Adversaries of God's Truth with me at the next Assizes,

which was on the 19**th of the first month**, 1662.

I shall pass by what befell between these two assizes, how I had, by my jailor, some liberty granted me, more than at the first, and how I followed my wonted course of preaching, taking all occasions that were put into my hand to visit the people of God; exhorting them to be steadfast in the faith of Jesus Christ, and to take heed that they touched not the Common Prayer, etc., but to mind the Word of God, which giveth direction to Christians in every point, being able to make the man of God perfect in all things through faith in Jesus Christ, and thoroughly to furnish him unto all good works. 2 Tim. iii. 17. Also how I having, I say, somewhat more liberty, did go to see the Christians at **London**; which my enemies hearing of, were so angry, that they had almost cast my jailor out of his place, threatening to indict him, and to do what they could against him. They charged me also, that I went thither to plot and raise division, and make insurrection, which, God knows, was a slander; whereupon my liberty was more straitened than it was before; so that I must not now look out of the door. Well, when the next sessions came, which was about the 10th of the 11th month (1661), I did expect to have been very roundly dealt withal; but they passed me by, and would not call me, so that I rested till the assizes, which was held the 19th of the first month (1662) following; and when they came, because I had a desire to come before the judge, I desired my jailor to put my name into the calendar among the felons, and made friends of the judge and high-sheriff, who promised that I should be called: so that I thought what I had done might have been effectual for the obtaining of my desire: but all was in vain; for when the assizes came, though my name was in the calendar, and also though both the judge and sheriff had promised that I should appear before them, yet the justices and the clerk of the peace, did so work it about, that I, notwithstanding, was deferred, and was not suffered to appear: and although I say, I do not know of all their carriages towards me, yet this I know, that the clerk of the peace (Mr Cobb) did discover himself to be one of my greatest opposers: for, first he came to my jailor and told him that I must not go down before the judge, and therefore must not be put into the calendar; to whom my jailor said, that my name was in already. He bid him put it out again; my jailor told him that he could not: for he had given the judge a calendar with my name in it, and also the sheriff another. At which he was very much displeased, and desired to see that calendar that was yet in my jailor's hand, who, when he had given it him, he looked on it, and said it was a false calendar; he also took the calendar and blotted out my accusation, as my jailor had written it (which accusation I cannot tell what it was, because it was so blotted out), and he himself put in words to this purpose: That John Bunyan was committed to prison; being lawfully convicted for upholding of unlawful meetings and conventicles, etc. But yet for all this, fearing that what he had done, unless he added thereto, it would not do, he first ran to the clerk of the assizes; then to the justices, and afterwards, because he would not leave any means unattempted to hinder me, he came again to my jailor, and told him, that if I did go down before the judge, and was released, he would make him pay my fees, which he said was due to him; and further, told him, that he would complain of him at the next quarter sessions for making of false calendars, though my jailor himself, as I afterwards learned, had put in my accusation worse than in itself it was by far. And thus was I hindered and prevented at that time also from appearing before the judge: and left in prison.

Farewell.

John Bunyan.

A Continuation of Mr Bunyan's Life; beginning where he left off, and concluding with the Time and Manner of his Death and Burial: together with his true Character, etc.

READER, THE PAINFUL AND industrious author of this book, has already given you

314

a faithful and very moving relation of the beginning and middle of the days of his pilgrimage on earth; and since there yet remains somewhat worthy of notice and regard, which occurred in the last scene of his life, the which, for want of time, or fear, some over-censorious people should impute it to him as an earnest coveting of praise from men, he has not left behind him in writing. Wherefore, as a true friend, and long acquaintance of Mr **Bunyan's** that his good end may be known, as well as his evil beginning, I have taken upon me, from my knowledge, and the best account given by other of his friends, to piece this to the thread too soon broke off, and so lengthen it out to his entering upon eternity.

He has told you at large, of his birth and education; the evil habits and corruptions of his youth; the temptations he struggled and conflicted so frequently with, the mercies, comforts, and deliverances he found, how he came to take upon him the preaching of the Gospel; the slanders, reproaches and imprisonments that attended him, and the progress he notwithstanding made (by the assistance of God's grace) no doubt to the saving of many souls: therefore take these things, as he himself hath methodically laid them down in the words of verity; and so I pass on to what remains.

After his being freed from his twelve years' imprisonment and upwards, for nonconformity, wherein he had time to furnish the world with sundry good books, etc., and by his patience, to move **Dr Barlow**, the then Bishop of **Lincoln**, and other church-men, to pity his hard and unreasonable sufferings, so far as to stand very much his friends, in procuring his enlargement, or there perhaps he had died, by the noisomeness and ill usage of the place. Being now, I say, again at liberty, and having through mercy shaken off his bodily fetters, – for those upon his soul were broken before by the abounding grace that filled his heart, – he went to visit those that had been a comfort to him in his tribulation, with a Christian-like acknowledgment of their kindness and enlargement of charity; giving encouragement by his example, if it happened to be their hard haps to fall into affliction or trouble, then to suffer patiently for the sake of a good conscience, and for the love of God in Jesus Christ towards their souls, and by many cordial persuasions, supported some whose spirits began to sink low, through the fear of danger that threatened their worldly concernment, so that the people found a wonderful consolation in his discourse and admonitions.

As often as opportunity would admit, he gathered them together (though the law was then in force against meetings) in convenient places, and fed them with the sincere milk of the Word, that they might grow up in grace thereby. To such as were anywhere taken and imprisoned upon these accounts, he made it another part of his business to extend his charity, and gather relief for such of them as wanted.

He took great care to visit the sick, and strengthen them against the suggestions of the tempter, which at such times are very prevalent; so that they had cause for ever to bless God, Who had put it into his heart, at such a time, to rescue them from the power of the roaring lion, who sought to devour them; nor did he spare any pains or labour in travel, though to remote counties, where he knew or imagined any people might stand in need of his assistance; insomuch that some, by these visitations that he made, which was two or three every year (some, though in a jeering manner no doubt, gave him the epithet of Bishop **Bunyan**) whilst others envied him for his so earnestly labouring in Christ's vineyard; yet the seed of the Word he (all this while) sowed in the hearts of his congregation, watered with the grace of God, brought forth in abundance, in bringing in disciples to the church of Christ.

Another part of his time is spent in

reconciling differences, by which he hindered many mischiefs, and saved some families from ruin, and in such fallings-out he was uneasy, till he found a means to labour a reconciliation, and become a peace-maker, on whom a blessing is promised in holy writ; and indeed in doing this good office, he may be said to sum up his days, it being the last undertaking of his life, as will appear in the close of this paper.

When in the late reign, liberty of conscience was unexpectedly given and indulged to dissenters of all persuasions, his piercing wit penetrated the veil, and found that it was not for the dissenters' sakes they were so suddenly freed from the hard prosecutions that had long lain heavy upon them, and set in a manner, on an equal foot with the Church of **England**, which the papists were undermining, and about to subvert: he foresaw all the advantages that could have redounded to the dissenters would have been no more than what **Polyphemus**, the monstrous giant of **Sicily**, would have allowed **Ulysses**, **viz.**: That he would eat his men first, and do him the favour of being eaten last: for although Mr **Bunyan**, following the examples of others, did lay hold of this liberty, as an acceptable thing in itself, knowing God is the only Lord of conscience, and that it is good at all times to do according to the dictates of a good conscience, and that the preaching the glad tidings of the Gospel is beautiful in the preacher; yet in all this he moved with caution and a holy fear, earnestly praying for the averting impending judgments, which he saw, like a black tempest, hanging over our heads for our sins, and ready to break in upon us, and that the **Ninevites'** remedy was now highly necessary: hereupon he gathered his congregation at **Bedford**, where he mostly lived, and had lived and spent the greatest part of his life; and there being no convenient place to be had for the entertainment of so great a confluence of people as followed him upon the account of his teaching, he consulted with them for the building of a meeting-house, to which they made their voluntary contributions with all cheerfulness and alacrity; and the first time he appeared there to edify, the place was so thronged, that many was constrained to stay without, though the house was very spacious, every one striving to partake of his instructions, that were of his persuasion, and show their good-will towards him, by being present at the opening of the place; and here he lived in much peace and quiet of mind, contenting himself with that little God had bestowed upon him, and sequestering himself from all secular employments, to follow that of his call to the ministry; for as God said to **Moses**, He that made the lips and heart, can give eloquence and wisdom, without extraordinary acquirements in an university.

During these things, there were regulators sent into all cities and towns corporate, to new model the government in the magistracy, etc., by turning out some, and putting in others: against this Mr **Bunyan** expressed his zeal with some weariness, as foreseeing the bad consequence that would attend it, and laboured with his congregation to prevent their being imposed on in this kind; and when a great man in those days, coming to **Bedford** upon some such errand, sent for him, as 'tis supposed, to give him a place of public trust, he would by no means come at him, but sent his excuse.

When he was at leisure from writing and teaching, he often came up to **London**, and there went among the congregations of the non-conformists, and used his talent to the great good-liking of the hearers; and even some to whom he had been mis-represented, upon the account of his education, were convinced of his worth and knowledge in sacred things, as perceiving him to be a man of round judgment, delivering himself plainly and powerfully; insomuch that many, who came mere spectators for novelty sake rather than to edify and be improved, went away well satisfied with what they heard, and wondered, as the Jews did at the Apostles, **viz.**: Whence this man should have these things; perhaps not considering that God more immediately assists those that make it their business industriously and cheerfully to labour in His vineyard.

Thus he spent his latter years in imitation of his great Lord and Master, the ever-blessed Jesus; he went about doing good, so that the most prying critic, or even Malice herself, is defied to find, even upon the narrowest search or observation, any sully or stain upon his reputation, with which he may be justly charged; and this we note, as a challenge to those that have the least regard for him, or them of his persuasion, and have one way or other appeared in the front of those that oppressed him; and for the turning whose hearts, in obedience to the commission and commandment given him of God, he frequently prayed, and sometimes sought a blessing for them, even with tears, the effects of which, they may, peradventure, though undeservedly, have found in their persons, friends, relations, or estates; for God will hear the prayer of the faithful, and answer them, even for them that vex them, as it happened in the case of **Job's** praying for the three persons that had been grievous in their reproach against him, even in the day of his sorrow.

But yet let me come a little nearer to particulars and periods of time, for the better refreshing the memories of those that knew his labour and suffering, and for the satisfaction of all that shall read this book.

After he was sensibly convicted of the wicked state of his life, and converted, he was baptized into the congregation, and admitted a member thereof, **viz.**, in the year 1655, and became speedily a very zealous professor; but upon the return of King

Charles to the crown in 1660, he was the 12th of **November** taken, as he was edifying some good people that were got together to hear the word, and confined in **Bedford** jail for the space of six years, till the act of Indulgence to dissenters being allowed, he obtained his freedom, by the intercession of some in trust and power, that took pity on his sufferings; but within six years afterwards he was again taken up, **viz.**, in the year 1666, and was then confined for six years more, when even the jailor took such pity of his rigorous sufferings, that he did as the Egyptian jailor did to **Joseph**, put all the care and trust in his hand: When he was taken this last time, he was preaching on these words, viz.: **Dost thou believe the Son of God**? And this imprisonment continued six years, and when this was over, another short affliction, which was an imprisonment of half a year, fell to his share. During these confinements he wrote the following books, viz.: **Of Prayer by the Spirit**: **The Holy**

City's Resurrection: **Grace Abounding**: **Pilgrim's Progress**, the first part.

In the last year of his twelve years' imprisonment, the pastor of the congregation at **Bedford** died, and he was chosen to that care of souls, on the 12th of **December** 1671. And in this his charge, he often had disputes with scholars that came to oppose him, as supposing him an ignorant person, and though he argued plainly, and by Scripture, without phrases and logical expressions, yet he nonplussed one who came to oppose him in his congregation, by demanding, Whether or no we had the true copies of the original Scriptures; and another, when he was preaching, accused him of uncharitableness, for saying, **It was very hard for most to be saved**; saying, by that he went about to exclude most of his congregation; but he confuted him, and put him to silence with the parable of the stony ground, and other texts out of the 13th chapter of **St Matthew**, in our Saviour's sermon out of a ship; all his methods being to keep close to the Scriptures, and what he found not warranted there, himself would not warrant nor determine, unless in such cases as were plain, wherein no doubts or scruples did arise.

But not to make any further mention of this kind, it is well known that this person managed all his affairs with such exactness, as if he had made it his study, above all other things, not to give occasion of offence, but rather suffer many inconveniences, to avoid being never heard to reproach or revile any, what injury soever he received, but rather to rebuke those that did; and as it was in his conversation, so it is manifested in those books he has caused to be published to the world; where like the archangel disputing with Satan about the body of **Moses**, as we find it in the epistle of **St Jude**, brings no railing accusation (but leaves the rebukers, those that persecuted him) to the Lord.

In his family he kept up a very strict

discipline in prayer and exhortation; being in this like **Joshua**, as the good man expresses it, viz., **Whatsoever others did, as for me and my house, we will serve the Lord**: and indeed a blessing waited on his labours and endeavours, so that his wife, as the Psalmist says, **was like a pleasant vine upon the walls of his house, and his children like olive branches round his table**; **for so shall it be with the man that fears the Lord**, and though by reason of the many losses he sustained by imprisonment and spoil, of his chargeable sickness, etc., his earthly treasure swelled not to excess; he always had sufficient to live decently and creditably, and with that he had the greatest of all treasures, which is content; for as the wise man says, **That is a continual feast**.

But where content dwells, even a poor cottage is a kingly palace, and this happiness he had all his life long; not so much minding this world, as knowing he was here as a pilgrim and stranger, and had no tarrying city, but looked for one made with hands eternal in the highest heavens: but at length was worn out with sufferings, age, and often teaching, the day of his dissolution drew near, and death, that unlocks the prison of the soul, to enlarge it for a more glorious mansion, put a stop to his acting his part on the stage of mortality; heaven, like earthly princes, when it threatens war, being always so kind as to call home its ambassadors before it be denounced, and even the last act or undertaking of his, was a labour of love and charity; for it so falling out that a young gentleman, a neighbour of Mr **Bunyan's**, happening into the displeasure of his father, and being much troubled in mind upon that account, and also for that he heard his father purposed to disinherit him, or otherwise deprive him of what he had to leave; he pitched upon Mr **Bunyan** as a fit man to make way for his submission, and prepare his father's mind to receive him; and he, as willing to do any good office, as it could be requested, as readily undertook it; and so riding to **Reading** in **Berkshire**, he then there used such pressing arguments and reasons against anger and passion, as also for love and reconciliation, that the father was mollified, and his bowels yearned to his returning son.

But Mr **Bunyan**, after he had disposed all things to the best for accommodation, returning to **London**, and being overtaken with excessive rains, coming to his lodgings extremely wet, fell sick of a violent fever, which he bore with much constancy and patience, and expressed himself as if he desired nothing more than to be dissolved, and be with Christ, in that case esteeming death as gain, and life only a tedious delaying felicity expected; and finding his vital strength decay, having settled his mind and affairs, as well as the shortness of time, and the violence of his disease would permit, with a constant and christian patience, he resigned his soul into the hands of his most merciful Redeemer, following his pilgrim from the City of Destruction, to the New **Jerusalem**; his better part having been all along there, in holy contemplation, pantings and breathings after the hidden manna and water of life, as by many holy and humble consolations expressed in his letters to several persons in prison, and out of prison, too many to be inserted at present. He died at the house of one Mr **Struddock**, a grocer, at the Star on **Snow Hill**, in the parish of **St Sepulchre's**, **London**, on the 12th of **August** 1688, and in the sixtieth year of his age,[11] after ten days' sickness; and was buried in the new burying place near the Artillery Ground; where he sleeps to the morning of the resurrection, in hopes

---

[11]   It is an established fact that John Bunyan died on Friday, August 31, 1688. He is recorded to have preached his last sermon on August 19.

of a glorious rising to an incorruptible immortality of joy and happiness; where no more trouble and sorrow shall afflict him, but all tears be wiped away; when the just shall be incorporated as members of Christ their head, and reign with Him as kings and priests for ever.

A brief Character of
Mr John Bunyan

HE APPEARED IN COUNTENANCE to be of a stern and rough temper, but in his conversation mild and affable; not given to loquacity or much discourse in company, unless some urgent occasion required it; observing never to boast of himself or his parts, but rather seem low in his own eyes, and submit himself to the judgment of others, abhorring lying and swearing, being just in all that lay in his power to his word, not seeming to revenge injuries, loving to reconcile differences, and make friendship with all; he had a sharp quick eye, accompanied with an excellent discerning of persons, being of good judgment and quick wit. As for his person, he was tall of stature, strong boned, though not corpulent, somewhat of a ruddy face, with sparkling eyes, wearing his hair on his upper lip, after the old British fashion; his hair reddish, but in his latter days, time had sprinkled it with grey; his nose well set, but not declining or bending, and his mouth moderate large; his forehead somewhat high, and his habit always plain and modest. And thus have we impartially described the internal and external parts of a person, whose death hath been much regretted; a person who had tried the smiles and frowns of time; not puffed up in prosperity, nor shaken in adversity; always holding the golden mean.

In him at once did three great worthies
shine,
Historian, poet, and a choice divine:
Then let him rest in undisturbed dust,
Until the resurrection of the just.

Postscript

IN THIS HIS PILGRIMAGE, God blessed him with four children, one of which, named **Mary**, was blind, and died some years before; his other children were **Thomas**, **Joseph**, and **Sarah**; his wife **Elizabeth** having lived to see him overcome his labour and sorrow, and pass from this life to receive the reward of his work, long survived him not; but in 1692 she died, to follow her faithful pilgrim from this world to the other, whither he was gone before her; whilst his works, which consist of sixty books, remain for the edifying of the reader, and praise of the author.

Vale.

FINIS

GT GRANDTYPECLASSICS.COM

"There is no friend as loyal as a book." E. Hemingway

1984 BY G. ORWELL

20,000 Leagues Under the Sea BY J. VERNE

A Christmas Carol BY C. DICKENS

A Doll's House BY H. IBSEN

A Hero of Our Time BY M. LERMONTOV

A Little Princess BY F. H. BURNETT

A Passage to India BY E. M. FORSTER

A Room with a View BY E. M. FORSTER

A Study in Scarlet BY A. C. DOYLE

A Tale of Two Cities BY C. DICKENS

Aesop's Fables BY AESOP

Alice in Wonderland BY L. CARROLL

Animal Farm BY G. ORWELL

Anna Karenina BY L. TOLSTOY

Anne of Green Gables BY L. M. MONTGOMERY

Anthem BY A. RAND

As a Man Thinketh BY J. ALLEN

Autobiography of a Yogi BY P. YOGANANDA

Beyond Good and Evil BY F. NIETZSCHE

Black Beauty BY A. SEWELL

Bleak House BY C. DICKENS

Candide BY VOLTAIRE

Common Sense BY T. PAINE

GTGRANDTYPECLASSICS.COM

"If a book is well written,
I always find it too short." J. Austen

Cranford BY E. GASKELL
Crime and Punishment BY F. DOSTOEVSKY
David Copperfield BY C. DICKENS
Dead Souls BY N. GOGOL
Devils BY F. DOSTOEVSKY
Dombey and Son BY C. DICKENS
Don Quixote BY M. DE CERVANTES
Dracula BY B. STOKER
Dubliners BY J. JOYCE
Eugene Onegin BY A. PUSHKIN
Far from the Madding Crowd BY T. HARDY
Fathers and Sons BY I. TURGENEV
Fear and Trembling BY S. KIERKEGAARD
Five Children and It BY E. NESBIT
Flatland BY E. A. ABBOTT
Frankenstein BY M. SHELLEY
Gargantua and Pantagruel BY F. RABELAIS
Gone with the Wind BY M. MITCHELL
Gorgias BY PLATO
Great Expectations BY C. DICKENS
Grimm's Fairy Tales BY J. AND W. GRIMM
Gulliver's Travels BY J. SWIFT
And many more...

www.ingramcontent.com/pod-product-compliance
Lightning Source LLC
Chambersburg PA
CBHW020445100426
42812CB00036B/3461/J